Study Guide

to accompany

Husted/Melvin
International Economics
Fourth Edition

prepared by
Steven Husted and Michael Melvin

 **ADDISON-WESLEY**

An imprint of Addison Wesley Longman, Inc.

Reading, Massachusetts • Menlo Park, California • New York • Harlow, England
Don Mills, Ontario • Sydney • Mexico City • Madrid • Amsterdam

Reprinted with corrections, November 1998

Study Guide to accompany Husted/Melvin, *International Economics, Fourth Edition*

Copyright © 1998 Addison Wesley Longman, Inc.

ISBN: 0-321-01761-7

3 4 5 6 7 8 9 10-VG-010099

Table of Contents

Chapter 1

An Introduction to International Trade

Summary and Review of Major Concepts

- The most common measures of economic activity in any country are the Gross National Product (GNP) or the Gross Domestic Product (GDP). Per capita GNP or GDP serves as a crude indicator of the country's standard of living. To obtain meaningful comparisons of these measures across countries, they must be converted to a common currency and adjustments need to be made for international differences in prices paid for goods and services.

- Important to the process of economic growth is the accumulation of knowledge and skills by workers. Competition through international trade provides a stimulus for workers to acquire new skills.

- All countries participate in international trade, importing and exporting goods and services to other countries. A rough measure of how much a country participates in international trade is reflected in its index of openness. This measure is calculated as the ratio of exports to GDP.

- Small countries tend to be more open--they aren't able to produce the wide range of products their citizens want to consume--and must export in order to obtain necessary imports. Large countries tend to be more closed--they are more likely to possess a variety of resources and factors of production--and thus are better able to diversify production and satisfy domestic demands.

- The United States is one of the most closed economies in the world, yet is also the world's largest exporter. Even though it sells huge amounts of goods and services abroad, its exports are small relative to the size of the overall economy.

- In general, international trade has become increasingly more important to the world economy with growth in world exports rising faster than overall output. The explosion in world trade is at least partly due to a reduction in the barriers to trade. This includes improvements in transportation and communications technology (and reductions in their costs), as well as lower government-imposed barriers such as tariffs and quotas on imports and exports.

- Although most countries maintain a rough equality between exports and imports, countries can and do run trade deficits or trade surpluses.

- The industrialized countries account for most of the world's exports (roughly 65% in 1995). Industrial countries are also the biggest importers of world exports.

- Asia's share of world exports has increased dramatically over the past quarter century, rising from 12% in 1965 to almost 30% in 1995.

- The United States is the major trading partner for many countries, reflecting its relatively large size and high income level.

- Countries tend to trade more extensively with their neighbors.

- The most important internationally traded products are automobiles, computers, petroleum, clothing, textiles, and electronic components such as transistors.

- In general, agricultural products, raw materials, semi-manufactured goods, and capital goods are more commonly traded than finished consumer goods. Two obvious exceptions are automobiles and clothing.

Define and/or Explain

Gross National Product (GNP)

Gross Domestic Product (GDP)

exports

imports

index of openness

trade deficit

trade surplus

Multiple Choice

1.   Which of the following questions are addressed in the study of international trade?

a.   How does international trade affect domestic unemployment and the level of earnings?
b.   Should a government apply tariffs, quotas or other barriers to trade?
c.   What type of goods is a country most likely to export?
d.   What type of goods is a country most likely to import?
e.   All of the above.

2.   Which item below is not included in the Gross National Product of France?

a.   The value of a new factory built outside Paris for a French manufacturer by a French construction company.
b.   A Japanese company's profits that come from manufacturing and selling bicycles in France.
c.   A French company's profits that come from operating an appliance factory in Thailand.
d.   The value of French champagne that is sold in Italy.

3 .   Which item below is not included in the Gross Domestic Product of France?

a.   The value of a new factory built outside Paris for a French manufacturer by a French construction company.
b.   A Japanese company's profits that come from manufacturing and selling bicycles in France.
c.   A French company's profits that come from operating an appliance factory in Thailand.
d.   The value of French champagne that is sold in Italy.

4.   The index of openness is the _____.

a.   ratio of imports and exports of goods and services to GDP (times 100)
b.   ratio of merchandise exports (not including services) to GDP (times 100)
c.   ratio of imports of goods and services to GDP (times 100)
d.   ratio of exports of goods and services to GNP (times 100)

5. As measured by the index of openness, which economy would you expect to be most open (try to answer this without looking up the numbers)?

a. Singapore
b. India
c. United States
d. China

6. As measured by the index of openness, between 1965 and 1994 most countries _____.

a. became more closed
b. became more open
c. stayed about the same

7. Comparing 1995 to 1950,

a. world exports were 500 percent higher and world output was 350 percent higher.
b. world exports were 450 percent higher and world output was 800 percent higher.
c. world exports were 1400 percent higher and world output was 500 percent higher.

8. The Kennedy Round and the Tokyo Round refer to _____.

a. bilateral discussions between the United States and Japan over international trade issues
b. international boxing tournaments
c. the development of quotas as government policy tools
d. multilateral negotiations in the 1960s and 1970s that resulted in the reduction of tariffs in industrialized countries

9. Choose the false response. In 1994, the United States _____.

a. was the world's largest importer
b. was the world's largest exporter
c. had the world's largest trade deficit
d. had the world's largest trade surplus

10. Which region of the world has seen its share of world exports rise over the past quarter century?

a. North America
b. Latin America
c. Asia
d. Africa

True or False?

T F   1.   For any country, GNP can be larger than GDP, but GDP can never be larger than GNP.

T F   2.   Per capita GNP or GDP tells us the average salary or wages earned by a resident of that country.

T F   3.   During the 1980s, GNP per capita rose more rapidly in low–income countries than in high–income countries.

T F   4.   Over the past four decades, world exports have grown at about the same rate as world output.

T F   5.   The United States is one of the most closed countries in the world, according to the index of openness.

T F   6.   The United States is one of the world's largest exporters.

T F   7.   Large countries are more open because their incomes are higher.

T F   8.   Most trade occurs in consumer goods.

T F   9.   We should expect world exports to roughly equal world imports each year.

T F   10.   Each country's imports must equal its exports each year.

6

Chapter 2

Tools of Analysis for International Trade Models

Summary and Review of Basic Concepts

- Economists build simplified models of economic activity in order to understand human behavior.

- Economic models can be verbal or mathematical, but must be consistent in their internal logic. The economic theories contained in a model are simplifications of more complex real world behavior. Certain assumptions are incorporated into the theories which eventually allow economists to make predictions about behavior. Theories can be rejected if they frequently fail to make correct predictions, or if they are correct less often than predictions based on alternative theories.

- Economists must be careful to distinguish between positive and normative economic analysis. Positive analysis is descriptive, or answers questions about what would happen, while normative analysis is prescriptive, telling us what should happen in a particular circumstance. Normative analysis involves value judgments about what ought to be.

- A model of international trade answers 5 important questions:
    why does international trade occur?
    what goods will a country import and what will it export?
    what will be the volume of trade?
    what will be the prices at which trade occurs?
    what will be the effect of trade on payments to the factors of production?

- Our model will be a general equilibrium model, meaning production, consumption, prices and trade will all be determined simultaneously.

- The basic assumptions of the model are as follows:

Assumption 1. All economic agents, particularly firms and consumers, exhibit rational economic behavior, meaning firms maximize profits and consumers maximize utility.

Assumption 2. There are only two countries (A and B) in the world, and only two goods (S and T). Each good is identical in each of the two countries, and some of each is always consumed in each country.

7

Assumption 3. There is no money illusion.

Assumption 4. Factor endowments are fixed and technology is constant in each country.

Assumption 5. Perfect competition prevails in both industries in both countries. There are no externalities in production.

Assumption 6. Factors of production are perfectly mobile between industries within each country.

Assumption 7. Community preferences in consumption can be represented by a consistent set of community indifference curves.

- In order to make rational economic decisions, economic agents must base their decisions on relative rather than nominal prices.

  If we know the price of good S is $10, before we decide to consume (or produce) it, we must also know the price of the alternative good T (suppose it's $5). The relative price of good S is given by the ratio, P_S / P_T. In this example the relative price of S is 2 (i.e., $10/$5 = 2). This means that S costs twice as much as T.

  If the absolute price of good S changes (suppose it rises from $10 to $12), we would need to know about any change in the price of good T before making any decisions about consumption or production. If, for instance, the price of T has also gone up, say $P_T = $6, the new relative price is the same as the old, and according to our model, behavior should remain unchanged.

- The price line, or terms of trade line, shows all the possible combinations of two goods (for a given relative price) that can be purchased with a fixed amount of money. The slope of the price line will be the relative price, or the rate at which one good can be exchanged in the market for the other. (Figure 2.1)

- A production possibilities frontier (PPF) graphically represents the maximum amount of output of one type of good that can be produced in a country for a given level of output of the other good, with technology and resources constant. Production can occur anywhere along or inside the PPF. If production occurs on the PPF, it is said to be efficient; if it occurs inside the PPF, then it is inefficient, since output of one or both goods can be increased without increasing the country's factors. Production cannot occur outside the PPF with resources and technology held constant. (Figure 2.2a)

- A curved PPF assumes that production of the two goods is subject to increasing opportunity costs. Stated simply, this means that production of each additional unit of one good requires the sacrifice of increasing amounts of the other good. (Figure 2.2a)

- Alternatively, a straight-line PPF assumes constant opportunity costs. In this case, the production of each additional unit of one good requires a constant, proportional decrease in the production of the other good, regardless of the level of output. (Figure 2.2b)

- Perfect competition in all markets and the absence of externalities insures that firms produce where price equals marginal cost; the marginal cost of a good is equal to the value of the resources used in its production; and that the market prices reflect the true social costs of production.

- Indifference curves represent the tastes and preferences of an individual. They have a number of important properties:

    (1) their location and shape are specific to each individual;
    (2) along an individual curve are various combinations of the two goods that the individual would be equally happy to have;
    (3) they are downward sloping reflecting the fact that if one good is reduced in the bundle the individual must be compensated with more of the other.
    (4) they are convex to the origin, meaning the more you have of one good, the less you value the next unit of it;
    (5) there are infinitely many indifferent curves lying one above the other, so that any two bundles can be compared;
    (6) preference rankings are always consistent, i.e., indifference curves can't intersect. (Figure 2.4)

- The autarky solution for an economy with constant opportunity costs (a straight line PPF) will occur at the point of tangency between the PPF and the highest possible community indifference curve, with relative prices always equal to the slope of the PPF. (Figure 2.5)

- The autarky solution for an economy with increasing opportunity costs (a curved PPF) will also occur at the point of tangency between the PPF and the highest possible community indifference curve, but relative prices will be equal to the slope of the PPF at the point of equilibrium production. (Figure 2.6)

- Real GDP may be used as a measure of welfare, but not nominal GDP. When real GDP rises, it means that more goods are available for consumption, and we have the potential to increase our collective satisfaction. An increase in nominal GDP can occur simply because prices rise, with no increase in potential consumption. (Figure 2.7)

- An increase in real GDP may increase a community's standard of living, if the rate of real GDP increases faster than the population grows. This means a community's per capita real GDP is rising. A rise in real per capita GDP, however, does not necessarily mean that everyone is better off. It is possible for some to experience gains while others' standards of living remain constant or even decline.

- A national supply curve for a product can be derived from the country's PPF and varying relative prices. As the price of the good rises, producers increase their output. The assumption of increasing opportunity costs results in a national supply curve that becomes steeper as output increases--greater price increases are needed to cover increasingly higher costs. (Figure 2.8a)

- A national demand curve for a product can be derived from the country's PPF and community indifference curves by varying relative prices. As the price of the good rises, new equilibrium consumption points occur where the highest CIC is tangent to the new relative price line. Given our basic assumptions, a country would want to consume less of a good as its price rises. (Figure 2.8b)

- Consider two countries with different national supply and demand curves so that their respective autarky equilibria will occur at different (relative) prices. The country with the lower relative autarky price for one good will have a comparative advantage in producing that good. The other country must by definition have a lower relative price for the other good and will have a comparative in advantage in its production. As long as countries have different relative prices in autarky, incentives exist for trade to develop along the lines of comparative advantage. Each country exports its comparative advantage good and imports its comparative disadvantage good.

- According to our model, the sources of comparative advantage in any particular good must lie in international differences in national demand or supply conditions.

Appendix 2.1

- A production isoquant represents different combinations of inputs that can be used to produce a certain level of output. With quantities of factors measured on the axes, isoquants that lie further from the origin represent higher levels of output. (Figure A2.1)

- Suppose a firm optimizes by maximizing output for a specific level of costs. The cost constraint can be drawn as a straight line with a slope equal to the absolute value of the wage-rental ratio, W/R. (Figure A2.2)

- The firm will maximize output at the point where the highest isoquant is just tangent to the cost constraint. This solution also indicates the optimal combination of inputs.

10

- Consider the production of two goods from two inputs within an Edgeworth box. Any single point in the box represents the allocation of factors between the two industries and indicates the two output levels. Factor allocations where the isoquants of the two industries are tangent to each other are efficient production points. At an efficient production point, it is not possible to reassign resources to allow increased output in one industry without lowering the output of the other.

- The "efficiency locus" is the collection of all efficient production points. (Figure A2.3)

Define and/or Explain

positive analysis

normative analysis

general equilibrium

money illusion

relative price

nominal price

production possibility frontier (PPF)

opportunity cost

indifference curve

community indifference curve

autarky

national supply

national demand

Multiple Choice

1. Terms of trade refers to

a. what goods are imported
b. what goods are exported
c. the volume of trade
d. the prices at which trade occurs

2. Which of the following can be used to build an economic model?

a. words
b. algebra
c. geometry
d. all of the above

3. Economic theories have all of these characteristics except

a. they abstract from reality
b. they use assumptions about the environment
c. the assumptions must exactly reflect the complexity of the environment if they are to predict accurately
d. they are necessarily simpler than the real world

4.   An answer to a descriptive question such as, "What would be the effect on US consumption of imported European beers if we imposed an additional 20% tariff on their import?" is called

a.   positive analysis
b.   normative analysis
c.   descriptive analysis
d.   prescriptive analysis

5.   An answer to a prescriptive question such as, "Since the consumption of alcohol is bad for our health, should we place an additional 20% tariff on beer imports?" is called _____.

a.   positive analysis
b.   normative analysis
c.   descriptive analysis
d.   prescriptive analysis

Questions 6 through 10 refer to Figure 1.

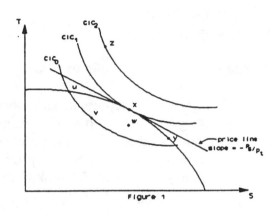

Figure 1

6.   Choose the true statement below:

a.   This person is indifferent between bundles u and y.
b.   Bundle z is better than bundles u, v, w, x or y.
c.   Bundle x is preferred to bundle z.
d.   Bundle x is just as good as bundle u.

7.   Of the six points (u, v, w, x, y and z) in Figure 1, feasible production points in this economy include

a.   only points u, v, w, x and y
b.   only points u, x, and y
c.   only points u, x, y and z
d.   only point z

8.   Of the six points (u, v, w, x, y and z), efficient production points in this economy include

a.   only points u, v, w, x and y
b.   only points u, x, and y
c.   only points u, x, y and z
d.   only point z

13

9.   Of the six points (u, v, w, x, y and z), equilibrium production and consumption will occur at

a.   points u, x or y
b.   point z
c.   point x
d.   point u

10.   In an economy like the one shown in Figure 1, when P_T rises and P_S remains constant, the price line

a.   becomes flatter
b.   becomes steeper
c.   shifts inward
d.   shifts outward

Questions 11 through 13 refer to Figure 2.

11.   In Figure 2, FE represents an economy's existing production possibility frontier (PPF). Suppose we discover a new supply of a factor that can only be used toproduce more S. What might the new PPF look like?

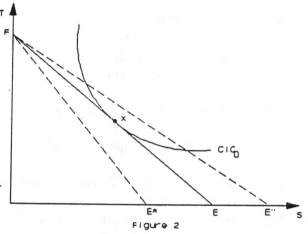

Figure 2

a.   FE
b.   FE*
c.   FE"
d.   two of the above

12.   Suppose that the relative price of S in this economy before the discovery was made was P_S/P_T = 2. What will happen to the relative price of S after the discovery?

a.   the relative price will stay the same
b.   the relative price will increase, $P_S/P_T > 2$.
c.   the relative price will decrease, $P_S/P_T < 2$.

13. Given the community indifference curve for the closed economy as shown, what would you expect to happen to equilibrium production and consumption of soybeans (S) and textiles (T) in this economy with the new PPF (after the discovery)?

a. production and consumption will remain constant at point x
b. production and consumption of both S and T will probably increase
c. production and consumption of both S and T will probably decrease
d. production of S will decrease while consumption of S increases; production of T will increase while consumption of T falls

14. The use of real GDP rather than nominal GDP allows us to

a. measure the value of output in a given year at constant prices
b. compare changes in real output rather than changes in prices
c. derive growth in per capita real GDP by subtracting the population growth rate from the growth in real GDP
d. all of the above

15. The national supply of good S as derived in Figure 2.8a in the text has an upward slope because

a. the production possibility frontier reflects increasing opportunity costs
b. higher indifference curves can be reached as the price of S increases
c. consumers prefer good S over good T
d. all of the above

True or False?

T F 1. In a closed economy, if equilibrium occurs inside the production possibility frontier, then consumers are not maximizing utility.

T F 2. An autarky solution refers to a model of an open economy trading internationally.

T F 3. In autarky, the optimal consumption point is not necessarily the optimal production point.

T F 4. In the autarky solution for an economy with constant opportunity costs, demand plays no role in determining relative prices.

T F 5. In the autarky solution for an economy with increasing opportunity costs, demand plays no role in determining relative prices.

T F 6. In the autarky solution for an economy with increasing opportunity costs, the relative price is the slope of the production possibility frontier (PPF) at the production point.

T F 7. In this same economy, the relative price is also the slope of the community indifference curve at the consumption point.

T F 8. If prices rise and production of all goods remains constant, then nominal and real GDP both rise.

T F 9. If prices rise and production of all goods increases, then nominal and real GNP both rise.

T F 10. An increase in real GDP always results in an increased standard of living.

Matching

_____ 1. $GDP = P_S \times S + P_T \times T$

_____ 2. $GDP/P_T = (PS/PT) \times S + T$

_____ 3. autarky

_____ 4. a price expressed in money terms

_____ 5. technical innovation, factor growth

_____ 6. describes what behavior should be

_____ 7. When community indifference curves are consistent, they have _____.

_____ 8. describes observed economic behavior

_____ 9. When Joe's income doubles, all prices double, but his spending pattern changes, he has _____.

_____ 10. a ratio of two product prices

a. relative prices
c. measures nominal GDP
e. measures real GDP
g. the properties of individual preferences
i. money illusion

b. positive analysis
d. closed economy
f. reasons a PPF might shift
h. normative economics
j. nominal prices

Chapter 3

The Classical Model
of International Trade

Summary and Review of Basic Concepts

- Adam Smith, David Ricardo, Robert Torrens, John Stuart Mill and others contributed to the classical theory of international trade, often referred to as Ricardian theory. Included in this theory was the fundamental concept of comparative advantage, which most economists since then believe determines the patterns of trade.

- By observing organization and production in factories, Adam Smith concluded that when each worker specialized in a certain task, the total output of the factory was greater than the sum of what each worker could produce on his own. He called this process the division of labor.

- Smith took this idea one step further--if countries each specialized in the production of a few goods, this international division of labor would lead to world production levels that would exceed the sum of what each country could produce in autarky. The surplus could then be divided between the countries, and all would have more.

- The governments of the time practised mercantilist policies designed to encourage exports and discourage imports. Smith argued, however, that the wealth of nations was measured by the quantity of goods and services its citizens enjoyed. Policies promoting the export of domestic goods while limiting imports actually lowered the wealth of a country.

- To develop our model of international trade, five more assumptions are added to the previous seven given in Chapter 2:

  Assumption 8. Factors of production cannot move between countries.

  Assumption 9. There are no barriers to trade in goods (including no transportation costs).

  Assumption 10. Exports must pay for imports (e.g. there is balanced trade).

The next two assumptions relate only to the classical model:

Assumption 11. Labor is the only relevant factor of production in terms of productivity analysis or costs of production.

Assumption 12. Production exhibits constant returns to scale between labor and output.

- Classical theory incorporates what is sometimes called the labor theory of value in price determination (assumption 11), where the price of a good is determined by the amount of labor it takes to produce it. In counting the amount of labor used, the labor to produce the physical capital employed in production must also be included.

- Constant returns to scale in production (assumption 12) means that a proportionate change in all inputs leads to an equi–proportionate change in output. With only one factor of production (labor), constant returns to scale yields an important characteristic of the classical model, the straight-line PPF. (Figure 3.1)

- Given the existence of perfect competition, the relative price of a good in autarky in a given country will be the absolute value of the slope of the PPF. This is simply equal to the ratio of the labor inputs for production of one unit of each good in that country. (Figure 3.2)

- When comparing the production of one good across two countries, the country with the lower labor input is said to have the absolute advantage in its production.

- If one country has an absolute advantage in producing one good and the second country has absolute advantage in the production of the other good, then each country should specialize in producing its absolute advantage good. By specializing in production and then trading with the other country, the two countries can each enjoy a higher standard of living than they would in autarky.

- If one country has an absolute advantage in both goods, it should specialize where it has the greatest absolute advantage. The other country should specialize where it has the least absolute disadvantage. This is the law of comparative advantage. By specializing in production and then trading with the other country, the two countries can each enjoy a higher standard of living than they would in autarky.

- When the two countries trade, a new international trade equilibrium results. There will be only one world price, called the terms of trade (TOT), which will be between the two original autarky prices. (Figure 3.3)

- While the TOT line will lie somewhere between the two original autarky prices, the actual price must be determined by forces of international demand and supply, known as reciprocal demand.

- Once a country specializes in production and trades at the international price, the TOT line represents all of the possible trading combinations. In other words, it represents the consumption possibilities frontier for that country.

- The new equilibrium consumption bundle with trade is the point of tangency of the country's CIC with the TOT line. The country's trade triangle incorporates the new equilibrium production point, consumption point and TOT line. For balanced trade between the two countries, the two trade triangles must be identical. (Figure 3.3)

- Since the new equilibrium in each country occurs at a higher CIC than in autarky, we know that each country must be better off with trade.

- We can also use real GDP to measure the gains from trade. Because the value of real GDP through the new consumption point exceeds the value of real GDP at the autarky consumption point, this verifies that the standard of living has risen. (Figure 3.4)

- The gains from trade come from two sources:
    consumption gains from trade occur because consumers can purchase some goods more cheaply on the international market;

    production gains from trade come about because production moves to the country's more efficient sector.

- Trade along the lines of comparative advantage can occur even when wages in the two countries differ. Trade will occur as long as the wage differential between the two countries does not exceed the maximum productivity differential.

- When technology leads to higher productivity levels, then the technologically advanced country must have a higher wage rate.

- If changes in wages exceed productivity increases, a country can lose its comparative advantage. The same result can occur if the exchange rate moves to the extent that the country's currency becomes overvalued.

Appendix 3.1

- The classical model can be extended to a world with two countries and many goods. As in the two good case, countries specialize in the production of the goods in which they have the greatest comparative advantage. The country that produces the intermediate range of goods depends upon the ratio of labor inputs and the relative wage rates in the two countries.

•　　A country's offer curve combines information from its PPF and CIC to show the country's desired imports and exports as the international terms of trade vary. When the offer curves of two trading partners are superimposed on the same graph, the equilibrium terms of trade, exports, and imports are determined by the intersection of the two countries' offer curves. (Figures A3.3, A3.4)

Define and/or Explain

division of labor

mercantilism

constant returns to scale

absolute advantage

comparative advantage

international terms of trade

consumption possibilities frontier

trade triangle

Walras' Law

reciprocal demand

importance of being unimportant

over and undervalued currencies

Multiple Choice

1.   All of the following individuals contributed to the classical theory of international trade in the late 18th and early 19th centuries except

a.   David Ricardo
b.   Robert Torrens
c.   Milton Friedman
d.   John Stuart Mill

2.   The classical, or Ricardian, theory of international trade explains

a.   how goods produced in high wage countries like the United States or Japan can compete in world markets with products produced in lower wage countries.
b.   how developed and developing countries can trade with each other and both benefit.
c.   how a country that is the more efficient producer of a good can benefit from not producing it but rather trading for the product with a less efficient producer.
d.   all of the above

3.   The increase in the level of world production that would occur when countries specialized in the production of just a few goods is based on the principle of

a.   the international division of labor
b.   Walras' Law
c.   mercantilism
d.   balanced trade

4.   According to classical trade theory, the labor theory of value means

a.   production of the same good in different countries requires the same labor input
b.   capital inputs are irrelevant to the cost of production
c.   labor inputs reflect constant returns to scale
d.   in autarky, the price of a good is determined by the amount of labor it took to produce it.

5.   Which of the following is <u>not</u> a characteristic of constant returns to scale in production in the classical model of trade?

a.   a fixed ratio between the quantity of labor employed in production and the amount of output produced
b.   each successive unit produced requires a larger input of labor than the last unit
c.   constant opportunity cost in production
d.   a straight line production function

6.   When it takes less labor input to produce a good in country A than in country B, country A is said to have

a.   absolute advantage in that good.
b.   constant returns to scale.
c.   comparative advantage in that good.
d.   division of labor.

7.   When country A produces both goods more efficiently than country B,

a.   country A should produce both goods and not trade.
b.   country A should specialize in its good of least absolute disadvantage.
c.   both countries would benefit from autarky.
d.   both countries can benefit from specialization and trade.

8.   The minimum information required to plot a country's PPF consists of

a.   the number of hours of labor in the economy
b.   ratio of labor inputs for S and T
c.   total available labor, labor required per unit of S, and labor required per unit of T
d.   total available labor and the ratio of labor inputs for S and T

9.   The slope of a country's PPF reflects

a.   the opportunity cost of S in terms of T
b.   the opportunity cost of T in terms of S
c.   both a. and b.
d.   none of the above

10.   Suppose two countries have labor inputs as represented in the table below. Based on the information in this table, Country B has

	Country	
	A	B
S	9	4
T	12	3

a.   absolute advantage in the production of both goods.
b.   comparative advantage in the production of both goods.
c.   absolute disadvantage in the production of S.
d.   comparative advantage in the production of S.

11. According to the table, country A has comparative advantage in the production of

a.   good S.
b.   good T.
c.   both goods.
d.   neither good.

12.   In this example, the equilibrium terms of trade could occur anywhere

a.   between 3/4 and 5/4
b.   between 3/4 and 4/3
c.   between 1/3 and 4/3
d.   between 1/2 and 3/4

Questions 13 through 15 refer to the figures below.

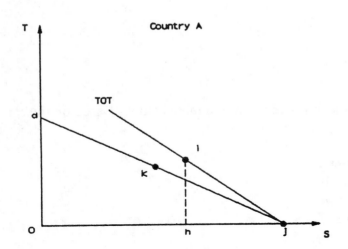

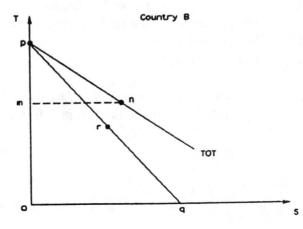

13.   Once trade begins, Country A specializes in the production of

a.   S.
b.   T.
c.   both goods.
d.   neither good.

14.   Once trade begins, Country A's trade triangle is

a.   jih
b.   koj
c.   doj
d.   npm

15.   With international trade, Country A consumes this amount of its own output.

a.   jh
b.   od
c.   hi
d.   oh

16.   Country B's exports are equal to

a.   om
b.   hi
c.   mn
d.   pn

The remaining questions refer to material contained in Appendices 3.1 and 3.2.

Suppose countries A and B have the industries in the table below, with the labor requirements specified for both countries

		Industry				
	J	K	L	M	N	P
Country A	3	6	7	1	4	2
Country B	4	2	6	1	5	3

17.   If the ratio of wages in the two countries (A/B) is equal to .9, then country B will concentrate on producing goods

a.   M, L, and K
b.   L and K
c.   N, P, and M
d.   P, J, and N

18.   If the ratio of wages is equal to .7, then country B will produce

a.   P and J
b.   only P
c.   L and K
d.   only K

19.   A country's offer curve is derived by varying this

a.   international prices
b.   the factors of production
c.   output

20.   and holding these elements constant

a.   the PPF, output, and consumption
b.   consumption and international prices
c.   total labor, output, and tastes

True or False?

T F   1.   Specialization in production in the classical model results in greater world output even though there are no new resources.

T F   2.   International price differentials that exist in autarky can persist in the trading equilibrium.

T F   3.   If a country has absolute advantage in both/all goods, there is no opportunity for gains from trade.

T F   4.   If a big country and a little country have the same pre-trade price ratio, there is no opportunity for gains from trade for either country.

T F   5.   If a big country and a little country have different autarky price ratios, then most, if not all of the gains will likely go to the smaller country.

T F   6.   When two countries open their economies to trade, the resulting terms of trade will always be the same as the larger country's pre-trade price ratio.

T F   7.   The farther the international price from a country's autarky relative price, the greater the gains from trade for that country.

T F   8.   When the wages in a country are higher than in another, all of the gains from trade go to the other country.

T F   9.   One country's trade triangle is congruent to its trading partners' trade triangle in equilibrium because exports must equal imports with balanced trade.

T F   10. If one country's trade triangle is larger than its trading partner's after trade begins, the terms of trade will change and the larger trade triangle will shrink as the economies move toward equilibrium.

Matching

_____ 1.   least absolute disadvantage

_____ 2.   classical theory

_____ 3.   exports equal imports

_____ 4.   constant returns to scale results in

_____ 5.   terms of trade line

_____ 6.   *The Wealth of Nations*

_____ 7.   *On the Principles of Political Economy*

_____ 8.   the most efficient producer

_____ 9.   encourage exports but discourage or prohibit imports

_____ 10.   all output can be reduced to a quantity of labor input

a.   Adam Smith
b.   David Ricardo
c.   Ricardian theory
d.   straight-line PPF
e.   mercantilism
f.   labor theory of value
g.   absolute advantage
h.   comparative advantage
i.   congruent trade triangles
j.   consumption possibilities frontier

Chapter 4

The Heckscher–Ohlin Theory

Summary and Review of Basic Concepts

- Although the classical theory explained much about patterns of international trade, the extreme nature of some of the theory's assumptions and conclusions conflicted with reality. For example, do we see much of current world trade conducted between countries at similar levels of economic development when the classical model predicts the opposite?

- In the early 20th century, Swedish economist Eli Heckscher and his student Bertil Ohlin laid out the foundation of a new theory of international trade, called the Heckscher-Ohlin (HO) theory.

- The HO theory was built around the observation of differences in the factors of production each country possesses and differences in the factors required to produce various goods.

- Heckscher and Ohlin argued that a country will have comparative advantage in producing the goods that require relatively large amounts of the factor with which that country is relatively well-endowed. For instance, since the United States has significant amounts of fertile farmland, it should have comparative advantage in many agricultural products.

- In addition to the insights the HO theory provides into the causes and effects of international trade, it also indicates the impact of international trade on factor prices; the effect of economic growth on the pattern of trade; and explains the political behavior of various interest groups in an economy.

- The formal structure of the HO theory retains the first ten assumptions from Chapters 2 and 3, drops assumptions 11 and 12 (used only for the classical theory), and requires five new assumptions:

Assumption 13. There are two factors of production, labor (L) and capital (K). Owners of capital are paid a rental payment (R) for the services of their assets, and labor receives a wage payment (W).

Assumption 14. The technologies available to each country are identical.

1 15. In both countries, the production of textiles (good T) always requires more ~~...~~ ~~a~~chine than the production of soybeans (good S). The production of both goods ~~...~~tries is subject to constant returns to scale.

~~...~~. Countries differ in their endowments of factors of production, L and K. We ~~...~~ that A is relatively capital abundant, while B is relatively labor abundant.

Assumption 17. Tastes in the two countries are identical.

- The capital (or labor) intensity of production (assumption 15) is a relative concept--that is, the total amount of capital (or labor) used is not important. Instead, we are concerned with the amount of labor required per machine. Constant returns to scale in the case of two inputs means it takes the same amount of labor and capital, in the same proportion, to produce the first unit as the last unit. Alternatively, if inputs of both labor and capital are doubled, output will double.

- Factor abundance is also a relative concept. A country is relatively labor abundant if the total labor force relative to total capital stock is greater than in the other country. Mathematically, if one country is relatively labor abundant, then the other country must be relatively capital abundant.

- From assumptions 15 and 16, the shapes of the production possibility frontiers can be determined. Since production of the two goods uses labor and capital in different proportions, the PPFs of both countries will reflect increasing opportunity costs; that is, they'll be curved instead of straight lines. (Figure 4.1)

- Since the community indifference curves for the two countries are identical (assumption 17), when the two countries are faced with the same relative prices and income (GDP), they will choose the same consumption bundle. This simplification means that the direction of trade will be determined solely by supply (production) conditions.

- The HO Theorem: A country will have comparative advantage in and should therefore export that good whose production is relatively intensive in the factor with which that country is relatively well endowed. This means that the country that is relatively labor abundant compared with the other country will have a comparative advantage in the good that requires more labor per machine to produce. Likewise, the capital abundant country must have comparative advantage in the capital intensive good.

- When the two countries begin to trade, each country will find the demand for its comparative advantage good will increase. As the relative price for its comparative advantage good increases in response to the increased demand, the country increases production of that good and reduces the production of its comparative disadvantage good. It can use the increased output of its comparative advantage good to trade for its comparative disadvantage good.

- When the two countries trade, a new international trade equilibrium results. There will be only one world price, the terms of trade, which will be between the two original autarky prices.

- The single international price that will prevail in equilibrium will be determined by the forces of international demand and supply known as reciprocal demand (see Chapter 3). The equilibrium price will be one that enables both countries to maintain balanced trade. As in the classical model, the countries' trade triangles representing desired trade flows must be congruent. (Figure 4.4)

- Incomplete specialization in production is the result of increasing opportunity costs. Once it begins to trade, a country will increase production of its comparative advantage good as long as the relative cost of expanding production is less than or just equal to the relative price.

- Differences between the classical and HO models include:

  Complete specialization always results in the classical model. Complete specialization is unlikely (although possible under certain conditions) in the HO model because of increasing opportunity costs in production.

  In the classical model, only demand conditions in the two countries affect the process of reciprocal demand. In the HO model, reciprocal demand leads to an equilibrium price through the impact of changes in both demand and supply. (Figure 4.5)

  The autarky price in the classical model is determined solely by supply conditions. In the HO model, autarky prices are determined through the interaction of supply and demand conditions.

- The Rybczynski theorem describes the effect of factor growth on a trading economy. It says that countries that save and invest little in new capital will tend to produce and trade goods with high labor content. Conversely, countries with high savings and investment rates will tend to produce and trade more capital intensive goods. (Figure 4.7)

- The factor price equalization theorem states that given all of the assumptions of the HO model, free international trade will lead to the international equalization of individual factor prices. Recall that higher wages can only be sustained in one country relative to another by maintaining higher productivity. Since the HO model assumes workers everywhere have the same productivity, trade guarantees that they earn the same wage. In reality, labor productivity differs widely across countries.

- The Stolper Samuelson theorem describes the effect of trade on the payments to factors. It says that competitive pressures of free international trade will benefit the abundant factor by raising the amount it is paid, while it harms the scarce factor by causing its payment to decline.

- Two implications of the Stolper Samuelson theorem are:

    We should expect scarce factors to lobby their respective governments for restricted trade since they stand to lose from trade.

    Although some factors lose from free international trade, the country as a whole gains from trade relative to autarky. (Recall that the new, post-trade consumption bundle is unattainable in autarky.) This means the winners must gain more from trade than the losers lose. Thus, it is possible for the winners to compensate the losers and leave all factors better off than they would be in autarky.

Define and/or Explain

factor endowments

labor (capital) intensive

labor (capital) abundant

incomplete specialization

factor price equalization

Multiple Choice

1.   Swedish economists Eli Heckscher and Bertil Ohlin

a.   were classical economists of the late 18th century.
b.   developed a new extension of the Ricardian model.
c.   laid out the foundation of a theory of international trade that differed from the classical theory in both its assumptions and results.
d.   used the assumptions of the classical model, but derived new and different results by using more advanced mathematical techniques.

2.   The Heckscher-Ohlin (HO) theory states

a.   a country should export the good with the highest output per unit of labor.
b.   a country will export the good that requires more intensive use of its abundant factor.
c.   a country should import the good that uses capital most intensively.
d.   a country should export the factor that receives a higher wage in the other country.

3.   If two countries had exactly the same factor endowments in addition to identical tastes, what trade patterns would occur according to the HO theory?

a.   trade would be determined solely by technology, with each country exporting the good for which it has a technological advantage.
b.   each country would export the good with the lower relative price.
c.   both countries would export the same good.
d.   the two countries would have the same PPF; there would be no gains from trade; and hence trade would not occur.

4.   Which of the following is characteristic of the HO model but is not characteristic of the classical model?

a.   straight line production function
b.   labor is the only factor of production
c.   trade triangles must be congruent
d.   incomplete specialization in production with trade

5.   Constant returns to scale means

a.   if you double the inputs, you will get twice the output.
b.   each unit produced requires inputs in the same proportion.
c.   the capital-labor ratio for the first unit produced and the last unit produced will be the same.
d.   all of the above.

6. Which of the following correctly describes a relatively capital intensive good?

a. the total amount of capital used in production is greater than the amount of labor required
b. the capital used per unit of labor is greater than for the other good
c. it uses a larger total amount of capital than the production of the other good
d. the value of the capital input is greater than the value of the labor input

7. A country is relatively capital abundant when

a. its endowment of capital relative to labor is greater than in the other country.
b. it produces capital intensive goods.
c. its endowment of capital exceeds the other country's capital endowment.
d. none of the above

8. The Heckscher Ohlin (HO) theorem

a. predicts or indicates the direction of trade between two countries.
b. says, in effect, that the capital intensive country will import capital abundant goods.
c. says that the labor abundant country will export labor intensive goods.
d. both a. and c.

9. Which of the following statements about the HO model is false?

a. In (trading) equilibrium, there will be a single international relative price.
b. Only demand conditions affect the equilibrium price, supply conditions are irrelevant.
c. The equilibrium price will be determined according to reciprocal demand.
d. Graphically, the international relative price (line) makes up part of the trade triangles of the two countries.

10. The Rybczynski theorem

a. says that a country with a high investment rate will tend to produce more capital intensive goods for its own use and will trade its labor intensive goods.
b. describes the effect of trade on the payments to factors.
c. says that a country with a high investment rate will tend over time to produce and trade more capital intensive goods.
d. states that free international trade will lead to the international equalization of individual factor prices.

11. The factor price equalization theorem

a. states that given all of the assumptions of the HO model (including equal labor productivity across countries), free trade will lead to equal factor prices.
b. proves that international trade theory has nothing to do with reality.
c. means that all factors will lose from free international trade.
d. both b. and c.

12. The Stolper Samuelson theorem

a. describes the effect of trade on the payments to factors.
b. says that scarce factors will gain from trade while the abundant factors will lose with trade.
c. implies that even though the abundant factor's payment decreases with trade, it is possible for the scarce factor (who gains) to compensate the losers and have all factors better off with trade.
d. all of the above

True or False?

T F 1. The HO theory states that trade is a result of differing labor productivity across countries.

T F 2. The HO theory is built around differences in factor endowments and different input requirements for each good.

T F 3. In the HO model, the assumption of identical technology in both countries would eliminate any basis for trade if applied to the classical model.

T F 4. Capital intensity can be measured just by knowing how much capital was used to produce a given output.

T F 5. In the HO model, both countries start with the same factor endowments.

T F 6. If country A employs a larger share of the world's capital stock than does country B, then A will export capital intensive goods to B.

T F 7. A curved PPF is the result of different factor endowments for the two countries.

T F 8. Increasing opportunity costs in production is the result of different factor proportions required for production of the two goods.

T F   9.   The Stolper Samuelson theorem gives us an explanation for why certain groups in a society are opposed to free trade.

T F   10.   The HO theorem means that when a country begins to trade, it will find increased demand for its comparative advantage good and will expand production of that good by cutting back on production of its comparative disadvantage good.

Matching

_____   1.   A country will have comparative advantage in and should therefore export that good whose production is relatively intensive in the factor with which that country is relatively well endowed.

_____   2.   If good X requires more labor per unit of capital than good Y, good X is _____.

_____   3.   If good X requires less labor per unit of capital than good Y, good X is _____.

_____   4.   According to the HO theorem, if a country exports labor intensive goods, its factor endowment must be relatively _____.

_____   5.   If country B has less labor per unit of capital than country A, country B is _____.

_____   6.   A country that invests little will tend to produce and trade more labor intensive goods -- is a consequence of the _____ theorem.

_____   7.   This common result of international trade in the HO model is extremely unlikely in the classical model.

_____   8.   Free trade will benefit the abundant factor by raising the amount it is paid, while it harms the scarce factor by causing its payment to decline.

_____   9.   The international equilibrium relative price is determined by _____.

_____   10.   Given the assumptions of the HO model, free international trade will cause these to become equal across countries.

a.   Stolper Samuelson theorem   b.   the HO theorem
c.   labor intensive   d.   capital abundant
e.   factor prices   f.   Rybczynski theorem
g.   labor abundant   h.   capital intensive
i.   incomplete specialization   j.   reciprocal demand

Chapter 5

Tests of Trade Models:
The Leontief Paradox and Its Aftermath

Summary and Review of Basic Concepts

- Economists test theories by locating data related to the theory they want to test and examining the data to see if the facts conform to the predictions of the model. Tests of the classical and Heckscher Ohlin (HO) models have been inconclusive and controversial.

- MacDougall tested the relationship between export performance and labor productivity in the classical theory by comparing US and British exports of 1937. First, he calculated the average products of labor (APL) for selected industries. Then he compared the ratios of the APLs and the ratio of wages in the two countries. According to the classical model, the US should export goods where its labor is relatively more productive than the ratio of wages, i.e. if wages in the US are double those in Britain, the US should export goods where its labor is more than twice as productive. He found that out of 25 products, 20 obeyed the general hypothesis. Note, however, that the classical model seeks to explain trade between two countries, which the test does not.

- In order to test the HO theory, Leontief used a tool called an input-output table, which describes the flows of goods and services between all industries. Using this framework, Leontief calculated the effect of decreasing US exports by $1 million while increasing imports by $1 million. He hypothesized that the United States, being capital abundant, should export capital intensive goods and import labor intensive goods. Thus, he expected relatively more capital per worker to be freed by decreasing exports than would be required to produce the goods to substitute for the decreased imports. In fact, he found US imports to be more capital intensive than US exports, a result known as the Leontief Paradox.

- Leontief made the first of many attempts to reconcile this paradox. He argued that his results were due to the assumption of equal labor productivity in the model, and that since American labor was so productive relative to workers in the rest of the world, the United States should really be viewed as relatively labor abundant. Studies since then, however, have shown that his claim that American labor was three times more productive may have been overstated.

- Vanek argued that the basic two-factor specification of the model was incorrect;in particular, it failed to recognize the role of natural resources. He argued that the United States is relatively scarce in natural resources, but relatively abundant in labor and capital. Furthermore, natural resources such as minerals tend to be produced by capital intensive techniques. In some recent tests taking this into account, the paradox disappears.

- Travis explained the paradox by the structure of US tariffs. US tariffs tend to be higher on labor intensive products, while tariffs of capital intensive items tend to be lower. This could lead to a distortion of US trade patterns away from comparative advantage and towards imports of relatively capital intensive goods. Since it is difficult to predict what US imports would have been in the absence of tariffs, the proposition is hard to test.

- Another possible explanation is that tastes are sufficiently different across countries to reverse the expected trade patterns. Evidence suggests that expenditure patterns and tastes differ between countries, but no one has been able to conclusively demonstrate they are sufficiently different to overturn the HO predictions.

- A final explanation comes from the methods Leontief used to test the theory. Rather than calculating the actual factor composition of US imports, he estimated the factor content by assuming that the imports would be produced with the same technology (Assumption 14) as the import competing goods produced in the United States. But, if factor prices are not equal, producers may substitute labor for capital, and imports may, in fact, be more labor intensive than comparable US-produced goods.

- In more recent tests of the HO model, Baldwin found the paradox applied to US trade for 1962, but Stern and Maskus examined 1972 trade data and found no evidence of the paradox. Tests on Japanese trade from the 1950s (when Japan was considered to be labor abundant) showed that Japanese exports were capital intensive and imports were labor intensive. However, given that Japan was more industrialized than some of its trading partners and relatively less industrialized than others, it would be expected to export capital intensive goods to some countries and labor intensive goods to others.

- There has been renewed interest in testing the HO model beginning in the 1980s due to two factors:

    Economists have realized that the tests undertaken by Leontief and others contained a conceptual flaw. Due to a lack of data, they tested the factor intensity of trade without linking these flows to the countries' factor endowments. Better data now allow us to test finer details of the theory.

    Leamer observed that when you have three factors (recalling Vanek's inclusion of natural resources) rather than two factors, then US exports might be relatively intensive in both the other factors, capital and labor. He showed that if the capital to labor input in the goods the US exported was greater than those goods Americans consumed, then the United States was revealed to be relatively capital abundant. To test this, Leamer studied the trade flows of 58 countries, measured the endowments of 11 factors for each, and compared these with the goods those countries trade. He showed that the relative availability of a given factor of production is important in explaining the goods that a country exports.

- The most recent empirical tests have shifted emphasis to explore modified versions of HO model that might be more consistent with real world experience. Daniel Trefler shows that if one allows for technological differences across countries, then there is considerable support for factor price equalization. In a second paper, he finds that combining the assumption of technological differences with an assumption that preferences in each country are biased toward domestically produced goods resolves much of the discrepancies between real world trade flows and those predicted by the HO model. In a similar vein, James Harrigan finds that a model that combines technological differences and factor endowments differences does a good job of explaining specialization in production across countries. Thus, a message of this work is that theoretical models that combine elements of the classical and HO models are supported by the data.

- Some economists have sought alternative theories of comparative advantage rather than attempting to reconcile the Leontief Paradox.

Human Skills: Keesing argues that differences in capital and labor are not as important as differences in endowments of skilled and unskilled labor. Specifically, he thinks that countries with relatively large endowments of highly skilled labor will have comparative advantage in products that are relatively intensive in skilled labor. Supporting this concept, Kravis found that the bulk of US exports are provided by high-wage industries.

Product Cycle Model: Vernon argues that some countries, such as the United States, have comparative advantage in inventing, developing and modifying goods (labor intensive activities). Over time, as the product becomes more standardized, production is automated (capital intensive activities), and the good can be efficiently produced in other countries and exported to the United States. Thus, the direction of comparative advantage may change over time.

Similarity of Preferences: While other theories have relied on factor endowments and differences in the costs of production to explain trade patterns, Linder focuses on the demand side. His hypothesis is that consumers prefer to choose from a variety of goods with slightly different characteristics, and that international trade allows us to obtain this variety. In fact, countries with similar standards of living will consume similar types of goods, and hence will likely be trading partners.

- Intraindustry trade occurs when countries export and import the same type of products. Although inconsistent with simple models of comparative advantage, examples are easy to find (e.g. computers, airplanes, cars).

- Some explanations for the occurrence of intraindustry trade are consistent with the HO model.

  Transportation costs. It makes sense for Western Canada to sell lumber to the United States, while Eastern Canada buys it from the United States.

  Poor data. Governments usually aggregate trade data into broad categories according to their end uses, even though goods with similar uses can be made in different ways (i.e. wooden or metal desks). In addition, categories often group dissimilar goods. For example, woolen jackets and cotton shirts are both included in the apparel category.

- Increasing returns to scale occur when a proportionate increase in the use of factors of production results in a greater than proportionate increase in output (or, the long run average cost curve falls as output increases).

- Increasing returns are external to an individual firm if the cost curves of all firms in an industry shift down as industry production increases.

- With increasing returns to scale, a country will find it advantageous to specialize and trade even if relative prices in international markets are the same as autarky prices.

- The pattern of trade with increasing returns is theoretically indeterminate and may be influenced by historical conditions.

- With increasing returns, countries may specialize in specific lines of differentiated products and then trade with other countries to provide consumers with a full menu of products. In this way, increasing returns give rise to intraindustry trade.

Define and/or Explain

input-output table

Leontief Paradox

product life cycle

intraindustry trade

increasing returns to scale

Multiple Choice

1. MacDougall's comparison of US and British exports of 1937 tested the relationship between export performance and labor productivity predominant in

a. the product life cycle theory
b. the HO theory
c. the classical theory
d. the theory of imperfect competition

2. According to the classical model as tested by MacDougall, the United States should export goods where its labor is relatively more productive than the ratio of wages. Specifically, if wages in the United States are twice those in France, the United States should export goods where its labor is

a. exactly four times as productive
b. less than twice as productive
c. just as productive
d. more than twice as productive

3. Leontief's test of the HO theory used

a. the assumption of dissimilar preferences
b. an input-output table
c. three factors of production
d. different technologies for production

4.   Leontief found

a.   equal labor productivity in the United States and Britain
b.   the United States to be abundant in natural resources
c.   US imports to be more capital intensive than US exports
d.   US imports to be more labor intensive than US exports

5.   According to Travis, low tariffs on labor intensive products combined with high tariffs on capital intensive goods

a.   could distort trade patterns away from comparative advantage
b.   could lead to the Leontief Paradox
c.   both a. and b.
d.   none of the above

6.   In Vanek's examination of the Leontief Paradox, he argued

a.   the United States was relatively abundant in skilled labor, but scarce in capital
b.   the HO theory could not be tested using real-world data
c.   the United States was relatively abundant in labor and capital, but relatively scarce in natural resources
d.   Leontief incorrectly measured labor productivity

7.   Leontief calculated the factor composition of US imports by

a.   assuming they were produced with the same technology as comparable goods made in the United States
b.   using input-output tables from countries exporting to the United States
c.   measuring foreign producers' inputs of labor and capital
d.   assuming US imports were labor intensive and that factor prices were equal across countries

8.   In his analysis of the HO model, Leamer observed that

a.   when there are three factors, then US exports might be relatively intensive in both the other factors.
b.   if the capital/labor ratio of US exports was greater than in the goods American consumed, then the US was revealed to be relatively capital abundant.
c.   both a. and b.
d.   none of the above

9. Some economists believe differences in capital and labor are not as important as endowments of skilled and unskilled labor. Comparative advantage based on human skills means

a. relatively low-wage countries will always have an advantage over high-wage countries.
b. countries with relatively large endowments of highly skilled labor will have comparative advantage in products that are relatively intensive in skilled labor.
c. both a. and b.
d. none of the above

10. Linder's hypothesis that consumers prefer to choose from a variety of goods with slightly different characteristics

a. can explain intraindustry trade
b. means that countries with similar standards of living will likely be trading partners
c. focuses primarily on the demand side of trade rather than on the supply side
d. all of the above

11. The existence of intraindustry trade

a. is inconsistent with the HO theory
b. can sometimes be explained by transportation costs
c. is impossible with imperfect competition
d. none of the above

12. Increasing returns to scale can explain

a. trade between countries with similar factor endowments
b. intraindustry trade
c. the role of history in shaping trade patterns
d. all of the above

True or False?

T F 1. The Leontief Paradox proves that the HO theory is wrong.

T F 2. Leontief showed that American labor is three times as productive as British labor.

T F 3. Tests of the HO model have found evidence of the Leontief Paradox in US trade data for 1962, but not for 1972.

T F 4. Tests on expenditure patterns have conclusively demonstrated that tastes are sufficiently different across countries to overturn the HO predictions.

T F 5. If a country is more industrialized than some of its trading partners and relatively less industrialized than others, it could be expected to export capital intensive goods to some countries and labor intensive goods to others.

T F 6. Detailed data on US factor endowments have shown the United States was most abundant in unskilled labor, followed by skilled labor, then physical capital.

T F 7. The same studies (as in 6.) found that US exports were most intensive in unskilled labor, followed by skilled labor, and then in physical capital.

T F 8. Poor performance of the HO model may depend on the unrealistic use of US input-output table to describe the technology used to produce US imports.

T F 9. Evidence presented by Kravis showing that the bulk of US exports are provided by high-wage industries shows Keesing's arguments on human skills are incorrect.

T F 10. Leamer's work on intraindustry trade strongly has prompted a revival of the classical theory of trade in recent years.

Chapter 6

Tariffs

Summary and Review of Basic Concepts

- Governments can take a variety of actions, called commercial policies, to influence the volume and composition of trade flows. These policies include tariffs, quotas, subsidies, and other nontariff barriers.

- Commercial policies generate costs and benefits for a society. Economists have developed tools to analyze the effects of commercial policies and the distortions they generate.

- Economies obtain both static and dynamic gains when they move from autarky to free trade. Static gains refer to increases in economic well-being, holding resources and technology constant. Dynamic gains refer to increases in economic well-being that accrue because trade expands resources of a country or induces increases in the productivity of existing resources.

- The static benefits of moving from autarky to free trade equilibrium can be divided into two parts: consumption gains and production gains. (Figure 6.1)

     Suppose the economy produces at the autarky production point, but is allowed to trade that output at free trade prices. The movement from the original community indifference curve to the new indifference curve on this price line represents the static consumption gains.

     Now let the production point move to its free trade equilibrium as well. The movement further out to this new community indifference curve respresents the static production gains.

- The dynamic gains from free trade refer to the relationship between trade and economic growth. These gains can arise in a variety of ways.

     If a country imports capital goods rather than consumer goods, it increases its productive capacity and is able to produce more of all goods. When it imports more capital goods than it would have produced in autarky, then trade raises the overall growth rate of the economy.

Trade enhances the diffusion of new technology between countries, which increases growth.

When trade raises the real income of an economy, this leads to higher levels of savings. In turn, higher savings mean there are more funds to invest and promote growth.

By allowing foreign firms access to local markets, free trade policy reduces the monopoly power of domestic firms. The added competition encourages more efficient production and discourages rent seeking.

Trade expands the size of the market and allows firms to more fully exploit any economies of scale.

- Trade can result in political benefits when countries become economically interdependent and are less likely to be hostile to each other.

- Tariffs are taxes on exports and/or imports. They can be collected as a percent of the value of the product (ad valorem), or as a flat fee per unit (specific). Compound tariffs have both ad valorem and specific components.

- Tariffs have two positive effects on the economy where they are imposed. The revenue effect refers to the money they raise for the government, and the protective effect refers to the protection they afford domestic producers.

- A tariff that is imposed when there is no domestic producer is a pure revenue tariff. An example would be an import tariff on cocoa in the United States since no cocoa is produced there.

- A tariff that is so high that no goods are imported is a prohibitive tariff. These are purely protective tariffs since no revenue is collected.

- Governments in developing countries often rely on tariffs as a source of government revenue. Developed country governments rarely rely on tariffs for revenue--they usually exist for their protective effect.

- Tariffs can also be tools of international policy. Countries can be punished or rewarded by the imposition or reduction, respectively, of tariffs levied against their goods. The United States (and other countries) grants some countries most favored nation (MFN) status, agreeing not to charge those countries a higher tariff than it charges any other country. Imports from countries without MFN status are charged higher tariffs.

- Developed countries can maintain lower tariff policies toward developing countries in order to encourage their growth. The United States and most other developed countries have instituted a Generalized System of Preferences (GSP) for developing countries in order to promote growth and industrialization.

- The economic analysis of the effects of a tariff are usually focused on the market for a particular good, incorporating a domestic demand curve and a domestic supply curve.

- The difference between what consumers would be willing to pay and the amount they actually pay is known as consumer surplus. Graphically, this is the triangular area under the demand curve and above the price line. (Figure 6.2)

- The difference between what the producers actually receive and the minimum amount they would accept in payment for their goods is known as producer surplus. Graphically, this is the triangular area above the supply curve and below the price line. (Figure 6.3)

- When a country moves from autarky to free trade and the free trade price of a good is lower than the autarky price, consumption will rise and domestic production will fall. Imports will make up the difference between consumption and production.

- Consumers of imports and similar local goods are better off with free trade than autarky because they can buy the product at a lower price and consequently buy more. Graphically, consumer surplus increases. (Figure 6.4)

- Producers of products that compete with imports are worse off with free trade because the lower price causes their profits to fall and may lead some to drop out of the market. Graphically, producer surplus decreases. (Figure 6.4)

- Note that consumers gain more than producers lose creating a net gain to the economy.

- When a country moves from autarky to free trade and the free trade price of a good is higher than the autarky price, consumption will fall and domestic production will rise. Exports will absorb the difference between consumption and production.

- Consumers of exportables are worse off with free trade because they now pay a higher price for the product, and consequently buy less. Graphically, consumer surplus decreases. (Figure 6.5)

- Producers of exportables are better off with free trade because the higher price induces some new producers to come into production while others increase the quantity they supply. Graphically, producer surplus increases. (Figure 6.5)

- But note that producers gain more than consumers lose, with a net gain to the economy.

- Since the country experiences net gains in the markets for both its imports and exports, it is clearly better off with free trade than it is under autarky. Graphically, this is equivalent to the movement to a higher CIC brought about by free trade. (Figure 6.1)

- When a tariff is imposed on an import, this raises the domestic price. Consumption decreases, marginal domestic producers now find it profitable to enter the market and total production increases. (Figure 6.6)

- A tariff causes a reduction in imports because (a) domestic output expands, and (b) domestic consumption falls.

- The exact magnitude of decreased imports depends upon the slopes (or elasticities) of demand and supply for the product in that country.

- Since consumer surplus falls more than the producer surplus and government revenues rise, there is a net welfare loss.

- The net welfare loss, or deadweight cost of the tariff, is the cost to society of imposing the tariff. It has two components (Figure 6.7):

    production deadweight cost, which is the cost of producting these new units in excess of the lower, international cost;

    consumer deadweight cost, representing the lost consumer satisfaction resulting from the shift in consumption to less desired substitutes.

- In the case of a small country and linear demand and supply curves the welfare cost of the tariff equals ½ × tariff × change in imports.

- Suppose the small country assumption is eliminated, and the country is a significant importer of the product. Because the country has market power, imposing a tariff could lead to a welfare improvement for the importing country. This gain comes as the tariff forces the supplier(s) to reduce the price they charge for their product in order to retain their export market. In this case, some of the burden of the tariff is shifted onto the exporting country.

- In the case of significant market power, an optimal tariff is the tariff rate that maximizes the sum of producer gains and tariff revenue minus consumer losses. Its size will depend upon the elasticities of demand and supplies.

- If retaliatory tariff measures imposed by the trading partner(s) or a trade war with multiple rounds of retaliation arises, then it is likely that any improvement in welfare brought on by an optimal tariff would vanish.

- The extent of a country's tariff protection can be measured by the height of its average tariff. This is the total tariff revenue for a given period of time, divided by the value of either total imports or total dutiable imports for that period.

- Average tariffs for developed countries tend to be relatively low--around 5%. Developing countries generally have higher average tariff rates, sometimes over 50%.

- The amount of protection a good receives from a tariff depends not only on its own tariff, but also on the tariffs on imported inputs used to make the good.

- The nominal tariff rate on a good might be very different from the true, effective protection afforded to a domestic producer. The effective rate of protection takes into consideration what proportion of the product is imported or produced domestically, and the effects intermediate good tariffs might have on the final product.

- The nominal rate of protection (NRP) = t/P, where t is amount of the tariff and P is the price of the product. The effective rate of protection (ERP) = $(v'-v)/v$, where v is the domestic value added under free trade, and v' is the domestic value added when tariffs are in place. The ERP is the amount domestic value added can rise relative to free trade levels.

- The imposition of tariffs on raw materials or intermediate goods can result in the domestic producer actually suffering from a negative ERP. A positive ERP throughout protected industries is generally assured through increasing tariffs by stages of processing, called tariff escalation.

Appendix 6.1

- Increased trade in final products rather than raw materials and intermediate goods leads to the likelihood that imports and domestic products are imperfect subsititutes. That is, they are treated as similar but not identical products.

- In this case, the imposition of a tariff on an imported good results in a higher price for the import and causes the demand for the domestic substitute to increase--the domestic demand curve shifts outward producing a higher domestic price.

- The higher price of the domestic good, in turn, has a residual effect on the demand for imported substitutes--the demand for imports also shifts outward.

- The total cost of this tariff is more difficult to estimate than in the case of perfect substitutes. In order to calculate the welfare effect of the tariff, we have to know (a) how far out the two demand curves will shift, and (b) the elasticity of supply for the domestic producer.

Define and/or Explain

commercial policy

tariff

quota

subsidy

nontariff barriers

static gains from trade

dynamic gains from trade

political gains from trade

ad valorem tariff

specific tariff

compound tariff

revenue effect

protective effect

Most Favored Nation (MFN) status

Generalized System of Preferences (GSP)

consumer surplus

producer surplus

deadweight cost of the tariff

optimal tariff

trade war

average tariff

effective rate of protection (ERP)

tariff escalation

Multiple Choice

Questions 1. through 6. refer to the Figure 1 at the right. The free trade relative price is PF.

1.   This country has comparative advantage in

Figure 1

a.   S
b.   T
c.   both S and T
d.   need more information to determine

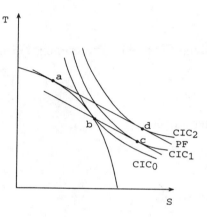

2.   The production point with free trade is

a.   point a
b.   point b
c.   point c
d.   point d

3.   If point b is the autarky production, then the movement from point b to point c represents

a.   the static production gains from trade.
b.   total gains from free trade.
c.   the static consumption gains from trade.
d.   none of the above

4.   If point b is the autarky production, then the movement from point c to point d represents

a.   the static production gains from trade.
b.   the dynamic gains from trade.
c.   the static consumption gains from trade.
d.   tariff revenue.

5.   When the community indifference curves are used as indicators of community welfare, the movement from CIC_0 to CIC_2 illustrates

a.   the one-time gains from the shift from autarky to trading at world prices.
b.   the total static gains from trade.
c.   an improvement in welfare.
d.   all of the above

6.   Dynamic gains from trade refer to

a.   the change in resource allocation as producers move from point b to point a.
b.   the natural increase in the supply of labor.
c.   the relationship between trade and increased economic growth.

Questions 7. through 13. refer to Figure 2 at the right.

7.   The consumer surplus gained by moving from autarky to free trade is represented by

a. $a+$b+$c+$d
b.   the distance gj
c. $a+$b+$c+$d+$e+$f
d. $e+$f

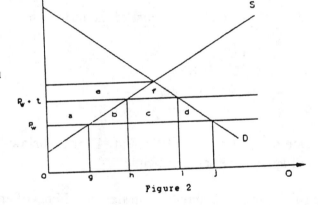

Figure 2

8.   The producer surplus lost by moving from autarky to free trade is represented by

a. $a+$b+$c+$d
b. $a+$e
c. $e+$f
d.   the distance gj

9.   In free trade, total imports will be

a.   the distance gj
b. $b+$c+$d
c.   the distance hi
d. $e+$f

10.   When a specific tariff of $t is placed on the item, compared to free trade consumers lose

a.   the distance gj
b. $b+$c+$d
c. $a+$b+$c+$d
d. $e+$f

11.   With the tariff, imports fall to

a.   the distance hi
b. $b+$c+$d
c. $f
d. $a+$b

12.   With the tariff, government revenue is

a. $c + $f
b. $c
c. $b+$d
d. $a+$b+$c

13.   The deadweight cost of the tariff is

a. $e+$f
b. $a+$b+$c+$d
c. $b+$c+$d
d. $b+$d

Questions 14. through 19. refer to Figure 3 below. Note that this example is not explained in the text, but applies the same principles.

14.   Figure 2 above illustrates the effects of an import tariff. Figure 3 illustrates the effects of

a.   an import quota.
b.   an export tariff.
c.   a compound tariff.
d.   an import subsidy.

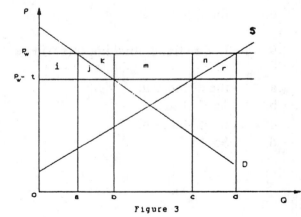

Figure 3

54

15. If P_W represents the world price, then $P_W - \$t$ represents

a. the domestic price for consumers and producers after the tariff is imposed.
b. the price of exports including the tariff.
c. the deadweight cost of the tariff.
d. producer surplus.

16. Because of the tariff, exports will

a. increase from bc to ad
b. decrease from ab to cd
c. decrease from ad to bc
d. stay the same at ad

17. Government revenue will be

a. $m
b. $k+$n
c. zero
d. none of the above

18. The net change in welfare due to this policy is

a. $m
b. $k+$m+$n
c. zero
d. -($k+$n)

19. Which of the following statements is true?

a. Consumers and the government gain more than producers lose resulting in a net welfare gain.
b. Producers lose more than the consumers and government gain resulting in a net welfare loss.
c. The government is imposing the optimal tariff.

Answer the remaining questions given the following information:

A domestic producer of gas-powered lawnmowers asks the government for and receives protection in the form of a tariff of $50 each on imports of gas-powered lawnmowers. The free trade price of each lawnmower is $200. Each domestic lawnmower produced requires $100 worth of imported components, on which there has always been a tariff of 10%.

20.   The domestic price of lawnmowers with the tariff will be

a. $150.
b. $200.
c. $250.
d. $260.

21.   The tariff on lawnmowers is

a.   an ad valorem tariff.
b.   a revenue tariff
c.   a compound tariff.
d.   a specific tariff.

22.   The nominal rate of protection on lawnmowers is approximately

a. $50
b.   20%
c.   55%
d.   25%

23.   The effective rate of protection on lawnmowers is approximately

a. $50
b.   20%
c.   40%
d.   25%

True or False?

T F   1.   A quota is a form of commercial policy.

T F   2.   Producers always gain from any type of tariff.

T F   3.   The producer surplus gained from an import tariff is always equal to the consumer surplus lost.

T F   4.   Static gains from trade take into consideration the effect of trade on economic growth.

T F   5.   Since trade increases real income, trade leads to higher levels of savings.

T F 6. The US government allows imports from Britain, France and West Germany under the Generalized System of Preferences (GSP).

T F 7. When a country moves from autarky to free trade, it experiences net gains from exporting goods and net losses from importing goods.

T F 8. Under certain circumstances, tariffs can raise a country's welfare.

T F 9. Developing countries generally tend to have lower average tariff rates than developed countries.

T F 10. Developing countries without significant market power often employ an optimal tariff.

Chapter 7

Nontariff Barriers and Arguments for Protection

Summary and Review of Basic Concepts

- Although tariffs remain the most universal form of commercial policy, the amount of trade subject to nontariff barriers (NTBs) is expanding rapidly. NTBs of particular interest that are discussed here include quotas, subsidies, health and safety standards, and government procurement policies.

- Quotas, either quantitative or value-based, limit the volume of goods traded between countries. A quota that eliminates trade in a product is an embargo. Embargoes are often placed on goods for political reasons.

- The rules of the World Trade Organization (WTO) prohibit import quotas on manufactured goods. Exceptions to this rule, however, are permitted in the case of temporary protection to aid distressed industries (referred to as safeguards protection, see Chapter 8), or for balance of payments problems. The WTO is currently overseeing the conversion of existing quotas on agriculture products and textiles into tariffs.

- Voluntary export restraint (VER) agreements are implicit quotas, whereby exporting countries agree to limit exports to a certain level.

- Unallocated global quotas, wherein no quota licenses are issued, are relatively uncommon because of the problems that arise in their implementation: they result in inefficient use of cargo facilities; some foreign producers may lose traditional markets with international frictions resulting; and successful importers can reap extraordinary profits.

- Quota licenses control the allocation of quota rights by giving the bearer the right to import specific goods into a country during a particular time period. These rights can be sold or given away. Their distribution determines the welfare impact of the quota system.

- The effect of a quota on the domestic supply of a good is equivalent to a horizontal shift outward of the domestic supply curve at the world price in the amount of the quota. Quotas serve to limit trade and raise prices, just as with a tariff. Consider the case of a tariff that has the exactly equivalent effect of a quota on prices and imports. The changes in consumer and producer surpluses will correspond identically, as will the deadweight costs. What was tariff revenue going to the government now becomes quota rent, profits that accrue to whomever owns the quota rights.

- Quota licenses can be auctioned by the government. Competitive bidding should result in the government collecting nearly all the rents. If this is the case, then the quota will have the same welfare effect as a tariff. In the real world, governments rarely auction quota licenses; instead it is common for governments to give them away to various groups.

- When quota licenses are given to domestic producers or importers instead of being auctioned, the quota rent accrues to domestic firms and becomes part of domestic producer surplus.

- When the licenses are given to foreign producers or exporters, however, the value of the quota rents is transferred to the foreign producers. In the process, the quota rents are added to the usual deadweight costs of protection, making such a policy significantly worse than alternative forms of protection. A voluntary export restraint (VER) is an example of this type of policy.

- Quotas have features that make them worse than equivalent tariffs.

- When a domestic monopolist faces a tariff, he can charge no more than the world price plus the tariff--trade ensures competitive behavior. Under a quota, however, the monopolist can exercise market power on the remaining part of the domestic market. A monopolist will charge higher prices and produce less under quota protection than under tariff protection.

- An increase in domestic demand in a market under tariff protection will be met by a rise in imports and the internal price will remain as the world price plus the tariff. With a quota prohibiting additional imports, prices will adjust upwards and deadweight costs will increase.

- Quotas also entail the administrative problem of how to distribute the quota rights. In the absence of an auction, they are often given away on the basis of traditional market shares, which does not allow consumers to alter their consumption choices.

- Quotas also tend to encourage more graft and corruption. Even if illegal activities are avoided, potential beneficiaries will spend money on legal forms of persuasion, such as campaign contributions or lobbying activities.

- Export subsidies are another type of NTB in the form of payments from a government to an export industry, usually based on the level of exports. This gives exporters a cost advantage over their international competitors. Export subsidies cause production to expand, draw resources away from the import competing sectors, and lead to a rise in the internal price of the good. In addition to paying more for the good at home, consumers become liable for the taxes to finance the subsidy as well.

- Forms of export subsidies include tax rebates, subsidized loans to foreign purchasers, insurance guarantees, government funding for research and development, guarantees against losses, direct grants or subsidized loans. US and international law both allow for countervailing duties against subsidized exports, to offset the subsidy and raise the price to pre-subsidy levels.

- Government procurement policies can be another type of NTB. In the United States, government agencies are required to purchase domestic goods and services unless the domestic price is more than 12% greater than the foreign price (50% greater for the Department of Defense).

- Health and safety standards can also be used to regulate trade in products. While such standards protect the health and safety of citizens, they can also provide a mechanism for protecting domestic producers if they are applied without legitimate justification on imported goods.

- Failure to protect intellectual property rights (IPR) can inhibit trade across borders when countries vary the degree of protection they offer. Moreover, some countries offer different levels of protection (sometimes none) to imported intellectual property than to domestically-produced products.

- Other NTBs include conditional import authorizations, variable levies that equalize import and domestic prices, price floors on foreign products, domestic content laws, currency undervaluation, and numerous forms of special treatment laws.

- Use of NTBs has increased dramatically. Imports of industrialized countries affected by NTB protection rose from 25 percent in 1966 to 48 percent in 1986. The greatest incidence of NTB protection is in foods and manufactures.

- Even these numbers underestimate the degree of protection. Many forms of protection are simply not included in the analysis, such as health and safety standards. Moreover, this total only includes trade that is completed, and does not estimate the trade that would have occurred without the restrictions.

Invalid Arguments for Protection

- Patriotism: Campaigns to "Buy American" may be effective marketing strategies, but in the case of protected industries, encourage actions that lower national welfare.

- Employment: The preservation of jobs in protected industries ignores protection's effects in other markets. The increase in output in protected industries must come at the cost of reducing efficient production in other industries.

- Fallacy of Composition: Protection is mistakenly justified on the grounds that because it is good for one protected industry, it must be good for all industries.

- Fair Play for Domestic Industry: The cry for "a level playing field" is often invoked to counter differences (i.e. advantages) in productive environments, such as lower wages, differences in pollution laws, etc. This denies domestic consumers the right to choose from the widest possible selection of goods in the marketplace, and cripples international trade's ability to enhance the competitive process.

- Preservation of the Home Market: Buying from home producers in order to keep the money and the goods completely neglects the benefits we obtain from imports. And imports must eventually be paid for by exports.

Valid Arguments for Protection

- In addition to the optimal tariff argument, there are a limited set of valid arguments for protection. In each case, however, there exist more efficient ways to achieve the same result.

- Government Revenue: We have seen that in the case of market power, tariffs enable governments to force foreign producers to pay the tax and raise welfare. Even without market power, however, many governments (particularly in developing countries) use tariffs to as a source of revenue because they are easy to collect. A more efficient policy that generated fewer costs would be an income tax.

- Income Redistribution: Trade policy can be used to redistribute income from one group in society to another. For example, tariffs are an example of income redistributed from consumers to producers.

- Noneconomic Goals: An outcome may be desired that is not directly related to economic welfare, such as national defense. National defense is often cited as a reason to protect industries from international competition. But protection is not the best policy to achieve the goal of a strong national defense. What industries merit protection? Can defense needs be better met by expanding imports? Direct subsidies to lower costs and free trade is usually a better policy.

- Infant Industry Protection: Temporary protection in order for an industry to establish itself and become efficient assumes protected firms will work to lower costs when, if successful, they must face foreign competition. It also implies governments are better able to choose viable industries than the private sector. Infant industry protection may be appropriate if there are desirable secondary effects, such as infrastructure development, that accompany an industry's development. Again, production subsidies with free trade will be more efficient than protection.

62

- Domestic Distortions: If there are distortions present in an economy that keep it from achieving perfect competition, then it may be optimal for governments to choose policies that add more distortions. For instance, protective policies in one sector may have secondary effects that require further protection to correct. Better policies would be to address directly the distortions that generated the need for protection.

- Protecting the Environment: Free trade may promote environmental degradation if polluting industries relocate to countries with relatively lax environmental laws. Trade restraints could discourage this relocation but would be inferior to a multi–country agreement on uniform environmental standards.

- In the specific case of the North American Free Trade Agreement (NAFTA), freer trade is not expected to significantly increase pollution in North America. Pollution abatement costs are not critical in the location decisions of U.S. manufacturers. Also, NAFTA will encourage Mexico to specialize in agriculture and labor– intensive manufacturing, which are relatively clean sectors.

- Strategic Trade Policies: The existence of increasing returns in an industry may be used to justify tariffs or subsidies. In some situations, trade policies impose no deadweight costs on either country, but simply capture monopoly profits that would have gone to foreign producers. It is difficult to know, however, whether to use a trade tax or a trade subsidy. Which policy is appropriate depends on subtle aspects of firm behavior. Moreover, use of these policies in one market may have secondary, and overwhelming ramifications in related markets. In any case, economists have not established that these are the best policies.

Define and/or Explain

quota

embargo

quota rents

voluntary export restraint

export subsidy

countervailing duty

Buy American Acts

infant industry argument

Multiple Choice

1.   Nontariff barriers (NTBs) include all of the following except

a.   quotas
b.   tariffs
c.   subsidies
d.   health and safety standards

2.   Which of the following is false?

a.   According to WTO rules, export quotas are generally prohibited.
b.   Quotas can be specified by quantity or value.
c.   An embargo is a quota set at zero imports.
d.   A voluntary export restraint is very different than a quota and has a dissimilar impact on welfare.

3.   Unallocated global quotas are relatively uncommon because

a.   they are prohibited by the GATT
b.   they are impossible to monitor and control
c.   they result in inefficient use of cargo facilities
d.   they are greatly preferred by exporting countries

4.   Quota licenses

a.   are illegal
b.   can be sold or given away
c.   eliminate the deadweight cost of a quota
d.   are sold in a voluntary export restraint

5.   When demand increases for a good subject to a quota,

a.   imports would stay the same but the price would rise
b.   the price would stay the same but imports would increase
c.   the supply curve shifts outward at the world price
d.   the price wouldn't change since imports ensure competition

6.   All of the following are forms of export subsidies except

a.   government-funded research and development
b.   tax rebates or tax credits
c.   insurance guarantees or guarantees against losses
d.   protection of intellectual property rights

7.   U.S. Government procurement policies

a.   require all agencies to purchase only domestic goods or services.
b.   allow all countries equal access to all government contracts.
c.   allow agencies to purchase imported goods if the US price of a product is more than 12% greater than the price of the foreign good.
d.   restrict the purchase of goods and services only by the Department of Defense.

Use Figure 1 to answer questions 8. through 12.

8.   Imports under free trade are

a.   ab
b.   bc
c.   bd
d.   ad

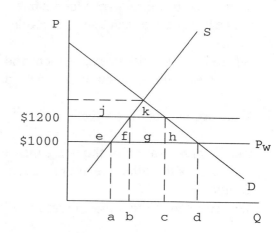

Figure 1

9.   A quota of bc units will cause
a.   the domestic price to rise by $200.
b.   the world price to fall by $200.
c.   government revenue to rise.
d.   two of the above

65

10. Domestic producers gain from the quota by the amount

a. $e
b. $e+$k
c. $f+$j
d. $f+$g+$h+$j

11. The quota rents are

a. $e+$f
b. $g
c. $g+$k
d. $f+$g+$h

12. Suppose the quota is replaced by a $200 tariff. The deadweight loss

a. would stay the same at $f+$h
b. would increase from $f+$j to $f+$h+$j
c. would decrease from $f+$g+$h+$j to $g+$h
d. would stay the same at $f+$g+$h

13. Quotas are most costly to domestic welfare when

a. quota licenses are auctioned by the government to the highest bidder.
b. quota licenses are given to domestic producers or importers.
c. quota licenses are given to foreign exporters.

14. The argument that protection increases total employment

a. is true because domestic producers would have to decrease employment if imports force them out of the market.
b. is true because foreign producers hire workers at lower wages.
c. is true because we then keep the products and the payment for the products in the domestic market.
d. is false because a rise in employment and output in protected industries can only come at the cost of efficient production in other industries.

15. Valid arguments for protection

a. include preservation of the home market.
b. may exist, although there are more efficient ways to bring about the same end result.
c. do not exist.
d. have resulted in the rapid increase in NTBs during the 1990s.

True or False?

T F 1. Voluntary export restraints are preferable to tariffs.

T F 2. Voluntary export restraints give quota rights to foreign producers.

T F 3. When quota rights are efficiently auctioned, a quota has the same domestic welfare effect as an equivalent tariff in the short run and in the long run.

T F 4. Sweden's financing the purchase of a new Boeing 747 through the US Export-Import Bank (known as the Exim Bank) at a favorable interest rate is an example of a US export subsidy.

T F 5. Removal of nontariff barriers is more problematic to policymakers because they tend to be product and country specific.

T F 6. A country should allow imports only from countries that agree to common international rules for trade.

T F 7. The Multifibre Arrangement (MFA) (controlling textiles and apparel imports) is a fair system and minimizes welfare loss by allocating quotas based on traditional market shares.

T F 8. According to the theory of the second-best, tariffs are the best way to counteract distortions in an economy.

T F 9. In industries with increasing returns to scale, tariffs, subsidies, or quotas may be effective ways of raising domestic welfare.

T F 10. The most important NTB's used by developed countries against imports from developing countries are dumping duties assessed against cheap foreign manufactured goods.

68

Chapter 8

Commercial Policy:
History and Practice

Summary and Review of Basic Concepts

- Since the end of World War II, general levels of trade barriers have fallen for many countries of the world. As a result, international trade has expanded rapidly. This trend toward trade liberalization has been spearheaded by the Western industrialized economies out of a desire not to repeat the pattern of trade wars and depression experienced prior to the war.

- Commercial disputes have risen as trade expanded, and have typically focused on trade in specific commodities. These disputes have often prompted lawmakers to change their trade laws or administration to fit changing circumstances.

- The U.S. Constitution gives Congress the explicit authority to regulate commerce with foreign nations, including the right to impose import tariffs. Over time, Congress has passed a number of tariff bills aimed at protecting specific industries or adjusting the general level of protection.

- The last tariff bill passed by Congress was the Tariff Act of 1930 (the Smoot-Hawley Tariff), which raised U.S. tariffs substantially and prompted the collapse of international trade. Most observers blame the results of this bill on the legislative process wherein localinterests took precedence over nationalwelfare. As a result, most trade bills since then have delegated authority to the President to negotiate lower U.S. tariffs in exchange for greater access to foreign markets. In addition, these bills have often tried to ensure specific indU.S.tries' ability to obtain relief from certain types of foreign competition.

- The first U.S. tariff act was passed in 1789. Its 5% import duty on most goods was intended to provide revenue for the federal government.

- The buildup to and the War of 1812 deeply affected U.S. tariff policy. The war (a) eliminated trade with Europe, and (b) led to high tariffs to raise money for the war effort. The resulting protection of the U.S. market greatly benefited U.S. manufacturers, who pressed for and won continued high tariffs after the war.

- Beginning in 1861, Congress increased tariffs several times in order to raise revenue to finance the Civil War effort. As after the previous war, however, tariffs remained high and did not fall until 1913. The post-World War I recession led to the Fordney-McCumber Tariff of 1922 which again heavily protected U.S. markets through higher tariffs.

- The Smoot-Hawley Tariff in 1930 was the last general tariff bill Congress would write. This classic example of logrolling and its aftermath of retaliatory tariffs succeeded in cutting the volume of international trade by two-thirds over the next four years (see Chapter 6).

- In 1934 Congress was persuaded to give the President the authority to negotiate mutual bilateral tariff reductions with the Reciprocal Trade Agreements Act. By 1945, tariffs had been reduced on average by 44%.

- The key principle of these bilateral negotiations was the use of unconditional most favored nation status. Under this rule, the U.S. would apply any tariff cut for one country to all other MFN trading partners.

- Following World War II, the General Agreement on Tariffs and Trade (GATT) was one of several international organizations created to deal with problems facing the postwar economies of the world. GATT's purposes were to (a) set rules for international commerce and (b) serve as a mechanism for (commercial) dispute settlement between countries.

- One of GATT's most important roles was to serve as a forum for multilateral negotiations lowering levels of protection. Two of the most successful rounds of negotiations were the Kennedy Round (1960s) and the Tokyo Round (1970s), which led to substantial reductions in tariff levels. The Uruguay Round (so named because the participants agreed at a meeting in Uruguay to begin negotiations) began in 1986 and was concluded in December 1993.

- One of the chief results of the Uruguay Round was the transformation of GATT into a new organization known as the World Trade Organization (WTO). The WTO is now responsible for setting rules not only for trade in goods but trade in services, international investment, and protection of intellectual property rights. The WTO also has a stronger dispute settlement procedure.

- Although Congress continues to delegate its authority to the President, it has passed successive trade bills restricting this authority, often to benefit specific industries. For example, domestic firms may seek repeals of tariff cuts under certain circumstances, and some concessions can be made contingent to political actions such as cooperation in drug control.

- Just as Congress has authorized the negotiated reduction in U.S. trade barriers, it has provided U.S. industries with alternative mechanisms to obtain relief from fair or unfair foreign competition.

- Dumping, or sales (by foreign firms) at less than "fair value," are prohibited. The principle aim of antidumping law is to place a floor on prices of imported goods. This protects domestic producers at the expense of consumers. A somewhat dubious justification for such laws is that they eliminate the possibility of predatory dumping--after driving the domestic producers out of the market by charging "unfairly low prices," foreign producers can begin to behave as monopolists.

- What is called dumping, however, is usually the result of rational economic behavior and need not be predatory. If an industry has market power in its domestic and foreign markets and faces different demand curves, it will rationally practice international price discrimination. Dumping can also result from government export subsidies to an industry.

- If a U.S. industry can show that it has been injured by dumping, it can have a special tariff applied to the dumped imports that is equal to the difference between the selling price and the fair market value (this price difference is known as the dumping margin). In order to receive this protection, a complaint must be filed with the Department of Commerce (DOC) (which investigates whether dumping has actually occurred) and the International Trade Commission (ITC) (which investigates the degree of injury). The industry receives temporary protection as soon as it files the complaint, which can then be adjusted or rebated upon final determination of the case.

- Congress views export subsidies (see Chapter 7) by foreign governments as an unfair trade practice, even if dumping does not occur, and provides countervailing duties (CVD) to offset the effects of the subsidy. CVDs do not require evidence of international price discrimination, and in some cases, no injury test is required.

- In addition to U.S. law, the WTO administers a subsidies agreement reached as part of the Uruguay Round negotiations. The agreement establishes three categories of subsidies: those which are prohibited; those which are actionable; and those which are non-actionable. Subsidies tied to export performance are prohibited and subject to dispute settlement.

- Section 301 of the Trade Act of 1974 provides the President with the authority to respond to unfair trade practices in foreign markets, that is, to counter actions of foreign governments in their own markets against U.S. firms. Specifically, he may impose import restrictions against any product of that country if an agreement can't be reached. Section 301 cases are administered by the USTR.

- Domestic firms can seek protection (through the ITC) from fairly traded foreign goods through the escape clause, which allows "temporary" restrictions on imports which threaten serious injury to the competing domestic industry. Protection is temporary in order to (a) slow the contraction of the domestic industry and ease the reallocation of resources, and (b) provide profits to domestic firms to reinvest in their industry so as to compete better.

71

- As an alternative to temporary import restrictions, the ITC can rule that workers or firms receive trade adjustment assistance (TAA) to help retrain and/or relocate workers.

- Other protective measures include restrictions (Section 337) against unfair patent or copyright infringement, price fixing, false labelling, false advertising, and trademark infringement; relief (Section 406) from market disruption by imports from communist countries; and restrictions on trade in goods considered vital to the national defense.

- Other countries have similar policies, especially industrialized countries. Antidumping statutes are common. There are efforts to protect industries threatened by fairly traded products (like the escape clause in U.S. legislation) known as safeguards protection. Much of the safeguards protection has increasingly taken the form of VERs. These actions together constitute a large share of the world's nontariff barriers.

Define and/or Explain

logrolling

unconditional most favored nation status

dumping

predatory dumping

international price discrimination

dumping margin

injury test

72

countervailing duty

upstream subsidies

Section 301

escape clause

trade adjustment assistance

safeguards protection

Multiple Choice

1. In general, since World War II the level of trade barriers in most countries has

a. fallen
b. risen
c. stayed about the same

2. The U.S. Constitution gives explicit authority to regulate commerce with foreign nations to

a. the President
b. the Congress
c. the Department of State
d. the U.S. Trade Representative

3.   The U.S. Constitution explicitly prohibits this type of commercial policy

a.   import tariffs
b.   export tariffs
c.   import quotas
d.   export subsidies

4.   U.S. tariff policy relied on a small tariff to generate revenue for the federal government until

a.   the War of 1812.
b.   the Civil War.
c.   World War I.
d.   the Great Depression and the Smoot-Hawley Tariff Act.

5.   Congress was persuaded in 1934 to give the President authority to negotiate trade policy

a.   so he could negotiate at the upcoming Tokyo Round.
b.   to avoid trade diversion.
c.   to prepare for World War II.
d.   rather than succumb to logrolling and more trade acts like Smoot-Hawley.

6.   Choose the false response. The WorldTrade Organization (WTO)

a.   calls for member countries to convert their tariffs to quotas.
b.   settles trade disputes between countries.
c.   organizes multilateral trade negotiations.
d.   establishes the rules for international commerce.

7.   Dumping

a.   by U.S. firms is prohibited by U.S. law.
b.   benefits domestic consumers and producers.
c.   can be rational economic behavior.
d.   allows foreign producers to behave as monopolists.

8.   Predatory dumping

a.   has never been proven.
b.   always results in trade diversion.
c.   by U.S. firms is prohibited by U.S. law.
d.   occurs when foreign firms sell their product below its fair market value.

9.   The application of countervailing duties (CVD) against subsidized exports

a.   does not require evidence of international price discrimination.
b.   does not require evidence of dumping.
c.   in some cases does not require an injury test.
d.   all of the above

10.   Resolution of dumping cases in the U.S. involve investigations by

a.   the Justice Department and the International Trade Commission.
b.   the Justice and Commerce Departments.
c.   the Justice Department only.
d.   the Commerce Department and the International Trade Commission.

11.   Section 301 of the Trade Act of 1974

a.   prohibits the import of subsidized goods.
b.   prohibits trade diversion.
c.   allows the President to act against unfair trade practices in other countries.
d.   contains the escape clause.

12.   According to Section 301, the failure of a government to give a copyright to a book by an American author while protecting the works of domestic authors

a.   results in trade diversion.
b.   is an adequate reason (legally) to restrict that country's exports of screwdrivers to the United States.
c.   merits use of safeguards protection.
d.   is an adequate reason (legally) to establish a VER with that country.

13.   The escape clause

a.   can be used to restrict the import of fairly traded goods.
b.   is designed to ease dislocation caused by contracting industries due to foreign competition.
c.   encourages firms to reinvest profits and improve their competitiveness.
d.   all of the above

True or False?

T F   1.   Prior to World War I, tariffs in the United States were always applied for their revenue effect and not for their protective effect.

T F   2.   The Fordney-McCumber tariff of 1922 was the last general tariff bill written by Congress.

T F   3.   After the disastrous effects of the Smoot-Hawley tariff, Congress gave the President the authority to negotiate tariff reductions with the Reciprocal Trade Agreements Act in 1934.

T F   4.   Congress has played no role in U.S. trade policy since it passed the Smoot-Hawley tariff.

T F   5.   In order for a country to legally trade with the United States, it must first obtain most favored nation status.

T F   6.   The GATT was created after World War II in order to regulate international exchange rates and facilitate balance of payments transactions.

T F   7.   The Nixon Round, the Taipei Round and the Paraguay Round are GATT-sponsored multilateral tariff negotations.

T F   8.   Congress has provided U.S. industries means to obtain relief from both fair and unfair foreign competition.

T F   9.   Dumping, especially predatory dumping, reduces consumer welfare.

T F   10.   The Office of the U.S. Trade Representative, the Department of Commerce, and the International Trade Commission all handle different requests for relief by U.S. industries.

Matching

_____ 1.   This part of the Trade Act of 1974 was unusual in that it gave the President authority to respond to unfair trade practices in other markets, not just in the United States.

_____ 2.   Measures that allow temporary restrictions on fairly traded imports that threaten injury to competing domestic industry.

_____ 3.   The organization that establishes common international trading rules.

_____ 4.   An alternative to temporary import restrictions, used to ease the reallocation of resources from contracting industries.

_____ 5.   Applied against imports subsidized by foreign governments.

_____ 6.   The import and sale of a good at a lower price than in the producer's market.

a.   escape clause
b.   countervailing duties
c.   dumping
d.   WTO
e.   Section 301
f.   trade adjustment assistance

Chapter 9

Preferential Trading Arrangements

Summary and Review of Basic Concepts

- In a preferential trading arrangement, participants agree to reduce or eliminate barriers to the movement of goods between member countries but retain trade barriers against nonmember countries. Such agreements are inherently discriminatory, in contrast to the principle of uniform treatment stressed by the WTO.

- A free trade area is a preferential trading arrangement in which each member reserves the right to decide what trade policy it will have regarding nonmember countries. The North American Free Trade Agreement (NAFTA) between the United States, Canada, and Mexico is a free trade area.

- In a customs union, members agree to harmonize their trade policies against nonmember countries. The European Union (EU) is a customs union.

- Preferential trading arrangements may or may not promote world efficiency.

- Inefficiencies arise when members are induced to shift the source of their imports from the lowest cost world producer to a higher cost producer from a member country. This is known as trade diversion.

- Preferential agreements are more likely to be welfare promoting if they lead to an increase in the overall volume of trade and cause high cost producers in some member countries to be displaced by lower cost producers from other member countries. This is known as trade creation.

- Another important source of efficiency gains involves economies of scale that may be exploited more fully when a larger market is created within the preferential trading area.

- For most of the past 50 years, the policies of the Mexican government discouraged economic integration with the rest of the world. Subsidies and import barriers were used to promote self-sufficiency in manufacturing. Heavy restrictions were placed on foreign investment in Mexico. The government also took on an important role in directing the economy through widespread ownership and control of Mexican companies.

79

- In response to massive inefficiencies in Mexican business and attendant problems with inflation and public debt, the government in the mid 1980s, under the leadership of President de la Madrid, took steps to liberalize the Mexican economy. Efficiency in domestic business was to be developed by promoting competition rather than restricting it. Trade barriers were reduced, regulations were eased, and businesses previously owned by the government were privatized. These reforms were continued by President Salinas who initiated the process leading to the North American Free Trade Agreement.

- Despite some political opposition, NAFTA came into effect in 1994. Political opposition in the United States came mostly from those who felt that U.S. workers would not be able to compete with lower paid Mexican workers. Other opponents included environmentalists who feared that with NAFTA, U.S. firms would relocate to Mexico in order to escape environmental regulation.

- Economic analysis suggests that neither fear is likely to materialize in a significant fashion. The agreement may bring hardship to certain sectors (labor–intensive manufacturing) and to certain labor groups (low–skill workers). Dislocation effects are not likely to be large in the short run. Mexico currently supplies only 2–3% of U.S. imports. Dislocation may become more severe over time, however, as resources are reallocated within Mexico toward export industries and as inflows of foreign capital and technology bolster the productive resources of the country. And, since environmental regulations add only a small fraction to the costs of production, and NAFTA should encourage Mexico to specialize in producing low pollution goods such as agricultural products.

- To date, NAFTA has had only a small effect on the U.S. economy. It not created major job losses in U.S. manufacturing. Although manufacturing wages are significantly higher in the United States than in Mexico, so too is the productivity of U.S. labor (see Chapter 3). Mexican labor productivity suffers from poor training, a shortage of managers, inadequate infrastructure, scarce capital and an unreliable legal system.

- The EU is the world's largest customs union. The ultimate goal of the EU is to eliminate all barriers to the movement of goods, labor, and capital within the union. It also hopes to establish a single European currency.

- The EU government consists of four main institutions.

    The European Commission initiates policy and ensures that EU law is applied by member states.

    The Council of the EU deliberates particularly important or controversial policy issues and also helps to oversee the execution of EU policy.

    The European Court of Justice decides the legality of Council or Commission acts.

80

The European Parliament is the legislative body of the EU and acts as the chief representative of the people.

• Important in the process of European economic integration was the 1987 Single European Act which called for a harmonization of technical standards and a deregulation of transportation and financial services. As of early 199, roughly 90 percent of the directives set out in the act had been enacted.

• At a conference in Maastricht, Belgium in 1991, EU members agreed to form a monetary union with a single currency by the end of the century. Members would have to cede sovereignty over monetary policy to a single EU central bank and closely coordinate their fiscal policies. Recent internal currency crises, however, have raised serious doubts about whether the monetary union can be completed by the targeted date.

• At the end of World War II, the United States was a leading proponent of multilateral trade liberalization and fought against a GATT amendment that would permit regional trading agreements. Beginning in the 1980s, the United States changed its position and negotiated regional agreements with Israel, Canada and Mexico. Some observers are concerned that increased emphasis on regional agreements will undermine WTO.

Define and/or Explain

free trade area

customs union

trade diversion

trade creation

North American Free Trade Agreement

rules of origin

Single European Act

Maastricht Agreement

Multiple Choice

Questions 1–5 are based on the following information. Car production is a constant cost industry (i.e., supply curves are perfectly elastic). Japan can produce cars for $12,000 each; the United States can produce them for $16,000; and Mexico can produce them at a cost of $20,000 each. In the questions below you are asked about the effects on the Mexican economy of a free trade agreement with the United States. To answer these questions, assume that Mexican consumers will buy 1 million cars per year if the price is $20,000 and that every $1,000 drop in the price generates an additional purchases of 100,000 cars.

1.   Before the free trade agreement, Mexico had a tariff on cars equal to $10,000 per car. What was the price of cars in Mexico before the FTA?

a. $22,000
b. $20,000
c. $16,000
d. $12,000

2.   Mexico signs the free trade agreement with the United States but retains the tariff of $10,000 on Japanese cars. What will the price of cars be in Mexico now?

a. $22,000
b. $20,000
c. $16,000
d. $12,000

3.	What is the change in Mexico's economic welfare in going from the situation in question 1 to that in question 2?

a.	$6.6 billion
b.	$4.8 billion
c.	$4.0 billion
d.	$3.2 billion

4.	Repeat the analysis in question 3 but assume this time that Mexico's tariff on cars is $6,000 instead of $10,000. What is the effect of the FTA on Mexico's economic welfare in this case?

a.	$ 2.6 billion
b.	-$4.6 billion
c.	-$4.8 billion
d.	-$7.2 billion

5.	Mexico's tariff is again $6,000. But now assume that U.S. production costs will fall to $13,000 per car if the U.S. auto industry can serve the entire North American market. What would be the effect of the FTA on Mexico's economic welfare in this case?

a.	$ 7.7 billion
b.	$ 0.5 billion
c.	-$1.2 billion
d.	-$5.4 billion

6.	Which of the following is not a part of NAFTA?

a.	elimination of tariffs on trade between the member countries
b.	more liberal rules regarding international investment in the countries
c.	free movement of labor between the countries
d.	establishment of a special commission to settle disputes between members

7.	Which of the following was not characteristic of Mexican economic policy from the end of World War II through the early 1980s?

a.	heavy protection of domestic manufacturers with import tariffs and quotas
b.	large scale government provision of social services
c.	widespread government ownership and control of Mexican companies
d.	liberal rules regarding foreign ownership of Mexican assets

8. Which of the following economic liberties are currently provided for in the European Union?

a. free movement of goods
b. free movement of capital
c. free movement of labor
d. all of the above

9. Which EU institution represents the Union in international trade negaotiations?

a. European Commission
b. Council of the EU
c. European Court of Justice
d. European Parliament

10. Which EU institution is the chief representative of the populace in setting EU policy?

a. European Commission
b. Council of the EU
c. European Court of Justice
d. European Parliament

True or False?

T F 1. Preferential trading agreements are relatively rare in today's world economy.

T F 2. Preferential trade arrangements are more likely to be welfare promoting if they lead to a significant increase in the overall volume of trade.

T F 3. Under the NAFTA, the United States and Mexico must agree on a set of common external tariffs they will apply to nonmember countries.

T F 4. NAFTA is the world's first free trade agreement involving both an advanced, industrialized country and a poor, developing country.

T F 5. NAFTA provides that no financial investment made by an individual or corporation from one member country may be seized by another member country without full compenstion.

T F 6. The United States will continue to lose manufacturing jobs to Mexico as long as Mexican wages are lower than U.S. wages.

T F   7.   A major achievement of Europe 1992 was to harmonize technical standards and regulations.

T F   8.   A goal of the EU is the unification of member country currencies into a single currency.

Chapter 10

International Trade
and Economic Growth

Summary and Review of Basic Concepts

- International trade can affect the level of economic growth of an economy. If the economy has been experiencing unemployment, then growth can come about with the reemployment of factors of production. If factors are fully employed, then economic growth requires new factors of production, or equivalently, technological innovation that allows existing factors to produce more output.

- One strategy for economic development is to encourage production and export of primary products such as agricultural products and natural resources. By expanding the size of the market through international trade, a country may be able to utilize its resources more fully. The development of an export sector may also expedite the process of building infrastructure.

- Some opponents of primary export-led growth argue that prices of primary products have been falling relative to prices of manufactured goods. Countries emphasizing primary products in their export program then may receive a declining share of the gains from trade. The statistical evidence on this issue is inconclusive.

- An alternative plan for economic development emphasizes import substitution. In this approach, a government erects high import barriers to encourage local production in selected industries. The rationale for the strategy is similar to the infant industry argument for protection.

- Drawbacks to import substitution are that the import barriers often remain well beyond the period that was originally intended and the system encourages citizens to expend resources to convince officials that their businesses are worthy of special protection.

- Countries adopting an outward looking growth strategy look to integrate their economies with the rest of the world. Policies include keeping domestic markets open to foreign firms; promoting efficient resource allocation by decontrolling wages and rents; and providing indirect subsidies to successful exporters. Examples of countries that have had success with outward oriented growth policies include Japan, Hong Kong, Korea, Singapore, and Taiwan.

87

- In economies with fully employed factors, growth can only result from factor growth and technical innovation. Variations in factor growth and technical innovation affect the manner in which a country grows, and will in turn, carry implications for the country's pattern of trade over time.

- Neutral economic growth occurs when the economy continues to produce and consume the goods in the same ratios as it did before growth. (Figure 10.2) Graphically, this requires:

  the new PPF must simply be a proportionate expansion of the old PPF

  consumption of all goods must increase equi-proportionately as income increases

- When growth results from an increase in the factor used intensively in export goods, then export production will tend to rise relative to the production of import competing goods, and by a greater percentage than the growth in GDP. This is called pro-trade biased growth. (Figure 10.3)

- When growth results from an increase in the factor used intensively in the import good, then the output of the importables will rise relative to export production, and by a greater percentage than the growth in GDP. This is anti-trade biased growth. In some cases, growth could actually lead to a switch in trade patterns.

- Technical change occurs when the same amount of output can be produced by fewer factor inputs, or when the same amount of inputs can produce greater amounts of output. Change can be described as neutral technical change, labor saving technical change or capital saving technical change.

- When a large country grows, increased output of the exportable or increased demand for the importable good could result in welfare-decreasing price changes. The country's terms of trade could change for neutral as well as biased economic growth. Pro-trade biased growth could worsen the terms-of-trade impact, while anti-trade biased growth could improve it.

- In an extreme case, biased growth could actually make a country worse off. If pro-trade biased growth of an exportable with inelastic demand is combined with a strong terms-of-trade effect, the magnitude of the deterioration in the country's terms of trade can lower overall welfare below the pre-trade level, resulting in immizerizing growth.

- A boom in a commodity can have surprisingly damaging effects on an economy that is abundant in this resource, a phenomenon known as the "Dutch Disease." A substantial price rise in a commodity will shift resources from the rest of the economy into the expanding commodity sector and could push up overall costs and damage the remaining sectors.

- International movement of factors (both labor and capital) is common. The migration of skilled and unskilled labor largely from poorer countries to the richer ones occurs regularly on legal and illegal, permanent and temporary bases.

- Capital moves across borders in the form of direct foreign investment (DFI), in which one firm acquires ownership or control of a foreign firm, or in the form of financial flows usually called portfolio investment. Firms that own or control firms in foreign countries are called multinational corportations (MNCs).

- Most employment in MNCs occurs in the manufacturing sector, both in the United States and overseas. Furthermore, nearly 70% of US multinational employment is in developed countries (Western Europe). Although MNCs face additional costs by operating in foreign markets, they may have special advantages such as access to technology (i.e. the secret formula for Coca-Cola), or face increasing returns to scale.

- The economic analysis of factor movements uses demand and supply curves. In the labor market, the demand for labor is determined by the value of the marginal product that labor produces. Diminishing returns to labor ensures that the demand curve will be downward sloping. Producers will hire workers until the marginal cost of the last worker equals the marginal revenue that accrues from that worker. In other words, firms will equate marginal revenue with marginal cost.

- Graphically, the rectangle formed by the price of labor (the wage) and equilibrium employment represents total payments to labor. The remaining triangle under the demand curve to the price line represents payments to the remaining factor of production, capital. The combined areas represent total labor income and total income paid to capital owners, or the value of GDP. (Figure 10.5)

- An increase in the supply of labor (immigration) will have a wage effect (the wage rate declines) and an output effect (total employment and output increases). Since labor earnings fall and the return to capital increases, there is also an income redistribution effect.

- In general, international factor flows tend to lower the incomes of those factors in the host country that most directly substitute for the factor and tend to raise the incomes of other factors. This helps to explain why governments institute policies that limit factor flows, such as restrictions on immigration and limits on capital outflows.

Define and/or Explain

economic development

89

primary export-led growth

import substitution policies

outward looking development strategy

neutral growth

pro-trade biased growth

anti-trade biased growth

neutral technological change

labor saving technical change

immizerizing growth

guest workers

brain drain

multinational corporation

marginal product of labor

diminishing returns to labor

value marginal product of labor

Multiple Choice

1. Which of the following is not typically found among the exports of developing countries?

a. food
b. petroleum
c. textiles
d. jet aircraft

2. During the late 1980s, the Mexican government initiated a development program that included a devaluation of the exchange rate, reduction of trade barriers, and liberalization of rules regarding foreign investment. This program is an example of

a. a primary export-led growth strategy
b. import substitution policy
c. export promotion policy
d. an outward looking development strategy

3. In an economy with fully employed factors, neutral economic growth requires

a. proportional expansion of the production possibility frontier
b. growth in the supply of only the scarce factor
c. the sum of the income elasticities must equal one
d. the increase in production must be greater than the increase in consumption

4.   Pro-trade biased growth requires

a.   GDP growth to be greater than growth of exportables
b.   income elasticity for the exportable good to be less than one
c.   import substitution policies
d.   an increase in the factor used intensively in the export good

5.   Anti-trade biased growth

a.   can lead to a switch in trade patterns
b.   can result from technological advances in the production of exportable goods
c.   can result from technological advances in the production of importable goods
d.   both a. and b.
e.   both a. and c.

6.   Suppose a capital abundant country with full employment achieves labor-saving technical change. It will most likely experience

a.   pro-trade biased growth.
b.   anti-trade biased growth.
c.   a switch in trade patterns.
d.   immizerizing growth.

7.   Most US multinationals are

a.   manufacturers located in low-wage developing countries.
b.   in the service sector.
c.   located in Japan.
d.   manufacturers located in Western Europe.

Questions 8. through 16. refer to Figure 1 below.

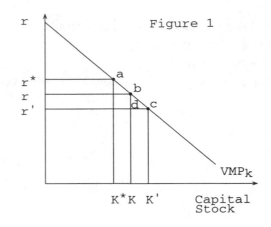

92

Figure 1 illustrates the demand for and supply of capital in a particular economy with restrictions on international factor flows. That is, goods can move freely across borders, but factors, such as labor and capital, are not allowed to move into or out of the country. The value of the marginal product of capital (VMP_K) represents the demand curve for capital, and OK is the supply of domestic capital.

8.   Suppose the government opens the economy to foreign investment. After the inflow of new capital, the domestic capital stock will be

a.   OK*
b.   OK
c.   OK'

9.   The new rental rate for capital will be

a.   r
b.   r*
c.   r'

10.   The total payment to owners of all capital will be

a.   OK*dr'
b.   fr*a
c.   OK'cr'
d.   OKbr

11.   Total payment to the (original) domestic owners of capital will

a.   stay the same at OKbr
b.   change from OKbr to OK'cr'
c.   change from OK*ar* to OK'cr'
d.   change from OKbr to OKdr'

12.   The total payment to labor will

a.   stay the same at rfb
b.   change from rfb to r'fc
c.   change from rfb to r*fa
d.   change from r*fa to r'fc

13. Will domestic labor be in favor of unrestricted foreign investment?

a. yes
b. no
c. not clear

14. Will the domestic owners of capital be in favor of unrestricted foreign investment?

a. yes
b. no
c. not clear

15. The value of GDP (not GNP) in this economy with foreign investment is

a. OKbf
b. r'fc
c. OK*af
d. OK'cf

16. Assuming the foreign capitalists take their rental earnings back home, the value of GNP is

a. OK*af
b. OK'cf - K*K'cd
c. OKbr + r'fc
d. OK'cf - adc

17. The "Dutch Disease" refers to

a. a commodity boom that brings about an overall economic downturn.
b. export promotion policies that fail in an economy with unemployed factors.
c. a decline in commodity prices that brings about overall economic growth

True or False?

T F 1. A government that encourages its citizens to purchase modern, imported products rather than traditional locally-made products is using import substitution policy.

T F 2. Examples of countries that had success with primary export-led growth include Canada and the United States.

T F 3. A key difference between export promotion and import substitution is that in the former, local producers are given incentives to serve a large world market and, therefore, may achieve greater economies of scale.

T F 4. When a large country grows, pro-trade biased growth could worsen the country's terms of trade.

T F 5. Anti-trade biased growth occurs when the rate of growth of production of importables is greater than overall GDP growth.

T F 6. When a trading country increases its factors of production and increases output, it is impossible for it to be worse off than it was before it grew.

T F 7. The "brain drain" refers to the intensive labor input required for some types of production.

T F 8. The marginal product of labor declines only in countries with unemployed capital.

T F 9. The value marginal product of labor (VMP_L) curve represents the demand for labor.

T F 10. The economic impact of international factor movements includes a factor payment effect, output effect, and income redistribution effect.

Chapter 11

An Introduction to International Finance

Summary and Review of Major Concepts

- The study of trade in financial assets is called international finance or international monetary economics.

- The balance of payments is a record of a country's transactions with the rest of the world.

- A trade surplus country exports more merchandise than it imports. A trade deficit country imports more merchandise than it exports. The United States has had a trade deficit since 1975.

- The exchange rate is the price of one money in terms of another. Monies are traded in the foreign exchange market. The greatest volume of foreign exchange trading occurs in London. London possesses the advantage of overlapping both Asian and American business hours.

- The foreign exchange market is the world's largest financial market. The U.S. dollar is the most popular traded currency.

- Purchasing power parity holds when 2 monies have the same purchasing power in 2 different countries. This would mean that goods would sell for the same price in 2 different countries when price is measured in a single currency (like that price of a hamburger in New York and Mexico City when the price is measured in U.S. dollars in each place).

- Interest differentials across countries reflect expected exchange rate changes. A high interest rate country typically has a currency that is expected to depreciate in value relative to the currency of a low interest rate country.

- Topics to be studied in international finance include: foreign exchange risk, since future exchange rates are not known; international investment, where we learn of the gains that may exist due to diversifying portfolios internationally; international monetary systems, where we review the history and present arrangements of international financial systems; international banking, where international lending and the Eurocurrency market is studied; and international macroeconomics, where the analysis of the equilibrium level of the national income, interest rates, and exchange rates is discussed.

Define and/or Explain

balance of payments

trade deficit

trade surplus

exchange rate

foreign exchange market

purchasing power parity

Multiple Choice

1.   The study of international trade in financial assets is called:

a.   international finance.
b.   international monetary economics.
c.   international trade.
d.   both a and b.

2.   A trade surplus occurs when:

a.   A country sells more merchandise to the rest of the world than it buys.
b.   Exports of bonds exceed bond imports.
c.   The balance of payments has a surplus.
d.   More money comes in to the country than goes out.

3.   The United States has had a balance of trade deficit since:

a.   1992.
b.   1987.
c.   1975.
d.   1951.

4.   The price in the foreign exchange market is called:

a.   the trade surplus.
b.   the money price.
c.   the exchange rate.
d.   the currency rate.

5.   Which country has the largest share of the global foreign exchange business?

a.   Japan
b.   the United States
c.   Switzerland
d.   the United Kingdom

6.   The most popular currency traded in the foreign exchange market is:

a.   the Japanese yen.
b.   the German mark.
c.   the Swiss franc.
d.   the U.S. dollar.

7.   If the price of a hamburger in Tokyo is ¥250 and the price of a similar burger is $2.50 in Chicago, what exchange rate (yen per dollar) would have purchasing power parity hold for the burger?

a.   10
b.   100
c.   25
d.   1

8. If the interest rate on a 12 month deposit in a U.S. bank is 5 percent and the interest rate on a comparable 12 month deposit in a Canadian bank is 8 percent, we would expect that:

a. no one will want to invest in U.S. deposits.
b. the U.S. dollar is expected to depreciate in value against the Canadian dollar.
c. the Canadian dollar is expected to depreciate in value against the U.S. dollar.
d. banks in Canada will have to stop offering such high interest rates.

True or False

T F 1. International finance is the study of international trade in goods and services.

T F 2. A country has a trade surplus when it buys more merchandise from the rest of the world than it sells.

T F 3. The balance of payments is a record of a country's payments made to its citizens.

T F 4. Monies are traded in the foreign exchange market.

T F 5. More foreign exchange is traded in Japan than in any other country.

T F 6. The U.S. dollar is the world's most popular traded currency.

T F 7. If the same lunch sells for $6 in San Diego and Ps48 in Mexico City, then if the exchange rate is 8 pesos per dollar, the lunch sells for the same price in each city.

T F 8. If the interest rate on a comparable investment in Japan and Germany is 2 and 4 percent, respectively, then: the Japanese yen is expected to depreciate in value against the German mark.

Chapter 12

The Balance of Payments

Summary and Review of Basic Concepts

- The balance of payments records a country's trade in goods, services, and financial assets with the rest of the world.

- Balance of payments data are reported annually for all countries. Developed countries usually report quarterly data as well.

- Balance of payments accounting is based on double entry bookkeeping--every transaction is entered as both a debit and credit on the balance sheet. Credit entries lead to inflows of payments or bring foreign exchange into the country. Debit entries lead to payments outflows or send foreign exchange out of the country. By definition, the sum of the credits and debits on all accounts will always be equal. In other words, the balance of payments always balances.

- For any given account, when the value of the credit entries is greater than the value of the debit entries, a surplus exists. When the value of the debits is greater than the value of the credits, a deficit exists.

- Summary measures are often used to evaluate the balance of payments. These measures "draw the line" at particular points down the listing of transactions that have economic implications. If we "draw the line" at the current account balance, all entries below the line are not included in the total. These items detail the transactions used to finance trade in merchandise, services, investment income and unilateral transfers.

- A current account surplus (deficit) implies that a country is running a net deficit (surplus) in the same amount below the line, so the country is a net lender to (borrower from) the rest of the world.

- $Y = C+I+G+X-IM$ or domestic GDP equals consumption plus investment plus government spending plus exports - imports (or the current account). This implies that national saving $= S = Y-C-G = I+X-IM$ or $X-IM = S-I$.

- The current account equals domestic saving less domestic investment. If $S>I$, then there will be a current account surplus ($X>IM$). For $S<I$, there will be a current account deficit ($X<IM$).

- **Measures of the balance of payments**

- *Balance of Trade*
  - net measure of merchandise trade
  - most commonly cited measure by the press, has more political than economic importance.

- *Balance on Current Account*
  - net merchandise, services, and investment income trade, plus unilateral transfers
  - provides a measure of the net change in a country's international financial position.

- *Basic Balance*
  - balance on current account plus long-term capital transactions; meant to emphasize long-run trends
  - Criticized on the grounds that (a) so-called long-term capital transactions include volatile portfolio items that have the same effect as short-term capital; and (b) short-term capital includes portfolio items that reflect long-run trends as well. Measure has limited usefulness and is not listed on the BOP table.

- *Liquidity Balance*
  - basic balance plus short-term capital, and errors and omissions; intended to put all the nonliquid liabilities above the line and liquid liabilities below the line, to measure the potential pressure on a country's international reserves.
  - Easily criticized since many nonliquid liabilities such as securities are instantly convertible into cash. For the United States, it does not reflect true pressure on reserves since the international demand for dollar holdings as foreign reserve assets does not put pressure on US reserves. Measure has limited usefulness and is not listed on the BOP table.

- *Official Settlements Balance*
  - the change in short-term capital held by foreign monetary agencies and official reserve asset transactions; for the United States, it serves as a measure of potential pressure on the foreign exchange value of the dollar.
  - Criticized on the same grounds as the liquidity balance, that there may be a demand for the dollar so that official stocks of dollars can build without there being any foreign exchange pressure.
  - Still considered useful, however, because changes in international reserves are an important determinant of a country's money supply.

- **Summary of Transactions Classifications**

- Capital account transactions impact the net creditor or debtor position of a country. A net debtor owes more to the rest of the world than it is owed, while a net creditor is owed more than it owes.

- The implications of the U.S. balance of payments position is quite different from most other countries. The United States can finance its current account deficits largely with dollars because of the demand for dollar-denominated debt or assets by foreign central banks. (By contrast, any current account deficit in Myanmar, formerly Burma, will put instant pressure on the government's international reserves because there is no demand for its currency [the kyat] as a reserve asset.)

- In principle, the current account balances of all countries should sum to zero. However, the global current account balance in recent years has summed to a deficit. This occurs because of problems in accurately measuring service and financial transactions.

- Is a trade deficit always bad and a surplus always good? No, the balance of payments must be analyzed in the context of other economic considerations. Deficits are not inherently bad, nor are surpluses necessarily good.

- Balance of payments equilibrium is a condition where exports equal imports (or credits equal debits) on an account such as the current account. Current account equilibrium means there is no need for financing, and the value of exports is just balanced by the value of imports.

- Equilibrium in the official settlements balance implies no change in a country's holdings of international reserves (i.e. short-term liquid assets held by monetary agencies). In a disequilibrium, reserve assets will flow from deficit countries to surplus countries and exert pressure on the exchange value of the relevant currencies. International reserves consist of gold, SDRs, and foreign exchange.

- The foreign exchange market can be portrayed using supply and demand curves. Suppose, for example, that the United States and Japan are the only countries in the world, and all reserves are held in foreign exchange. In the yen market, the supply of yen results from U.S. sales of goods or financial assets to Japan. The demand for yen comes from U.S. purchases goods or financial assets from Japan. At the equilibrium price (the exchange rate), the demand and supply for yen are equal.

- When the demand for and/or the supply of yen changes, maintenance of the old exchange rate (a fixed exchange rate) means reserves must flow between the two countries. When currency values are determined by market forces, equilibrium is restored by a change in the exchange rate.

- Many countries that wish to maintain a fixed exchange rate but lack sufficient reserves resort to direct controls. In these cases, the supply and demand curves are manipulated by the government by implementing quotas or fixing prices to force a balance of payments equilibrium.

Define and/or Explain

deficit (surplus)

balance of trade

basic balance

liquidity balance

official settlements balance

balance of payments equilibrium

flexible exchange rates

fixed exchange rates

Multiple Choice

1. The balance of payments

a. must sum to zero in the end, by definition.
b. records a country's trade in goods, services and financial assets with the rest of the world.
c. requires two entries for each transaction.
d. (a.) and (b.) only.
e. (a.), (b.) and (c.).

2. Which of the following would not be included in the U.S. current account?

a. the interest I receive on my British bonds
b. purchase of a 90-day U.S. Treasury Bill by a German
c. purchase of chemicals by a Brazilian
d. the money I spend on my trip to Australia

3. A unilateral transfer is

a. migration into or out of the country.
b. where you "draw the line".
c. birthday money from your aunt who lives in Thailand.
d. part of the capital account but not the current account.

4. A current account deficit

a. implies the country is a net borrower with the rest of the world.
b. is always bad.
c. implies a matching capital account deficit.
d. is very rare for most countries.

5. The United States has experienced current account deficits every year since

a. 1958
b. 1964
c. 1977
d. 1982

6. In balance of payments accounting, a credit

a. is entered for exported goods
b. sends foreign exchange out of the country
c. results in a demand for foreign exchange
d. none of the above

7. When we "draw the line" in the balance of payments

a. we determine the exchange rate.
b. we sum the items above the line, which are financed by transactions below the line.
c. we ration foreign exchange.
d. we deduct foreign aid from the current account.

8. The balance of payments (in the United States) is reported by

a. the Treasury Department.
b. the United States Trade Representative (USTR).
c. the Department of Commerce.
d. the Department of State.

9. Which of the following balances is not reported in the official U.S. balance of payments?

a. the trade balance
b. the balance on current account
c. the basic balance
d. the balance on goods and services

10. All of the following are international reserves except

a. SDRs.
b. gold.
c. foreign credits not yet received.
d. foreign exchange.

11. If the official settlements balance of payments equals zero,

a. then the current and capital accounts exactly balance.
b. there will be a tendency for the currency to depreciate.
c. then there must be a flexible exchange rate.
d. there will be a tendency for the currency to appreciate.

12. X-IM =

a. I+C
b. C+I+G+Y
c. S-I
d. C-G

13. Reducing a current account deficit requires

a. increasing domestic saving relative to investment.
b. decreasing domestic tax revenues relative to government spending.
c. increasing a capital account surplus.
d. reducing national output relative to national spending.

True or False?

T F 1. The balance of payments is based on double-entry bookkeeping.

T F 2. The U.S. current account deficit since the early 1980s has mostly been financed by foreign official capital inflows.

T F 3. For any particular account, a surplus exists when the value of the debit entries exceeds the value of the credit entries.

T F 4. The current account consists of the value of trade in goods and services, plus unilateral transfers.

T F 5. Even though the United States has maintained current account deficits in recent years, the United States is a net international creditor.

T F 6. If the value of foreign interest and dividends to U.S. citizens is large enough, it is possible to have both a balance of trade deficit and a current account surplus.

T F 7. When a country runs a current account deficit, then it consumes more at home than is produced there.

T F 8. With floating exchange rates, the balance of payments equilibrium is restored by exchange rate changes.

T F 9. If national saving falls relative to national investment, the current account deficit will increase.

T F   10.   Balance of payments accounting is a complete statement of all official transactions, but not private transactions.

Matching

Consider the following transactions in the U.S. balance of payments. Choose the corresponding transactions classifications from the list of possible entries below. Note there will be two answers for each transaction, and there may be duplicate entries. (C stands for credit, D for debit.)

C   D

_____ _____   1.   Mexico pays $5 million in interest to the Bank of America in San Francisco for interest on a loan.

_____ _____   2.   Texas Instruments buys a $6 million plant in Singapore. It pays for it with a check drawn on a Hong Kong bank.

_____ _____   3.   The United States gives Egypt $3 million in foreign aid for agricultural improvements. The grant is funded by creating a $3 million deposit for Egypt in a U.S. bank.

_____ _____   4.   The Egyptian government buys $2.5 million of tractors and other equipment from U.S. manufacturers. Payment is made from the bank deposit created in (3).

_____ _____   5.   The Egyptian government buys a 90-day U.S. Treasury Bill with the remaining $.5 million.

possible answers:

	credits	debits
merchandise (goods)	a.	b.
services	c.	d.
investment income	e.	f.
unilateral transfer	g.	h.
short-term capital	i.	j.
long-term capital	k.	l.

Chapter 13

The Foreign Exchange Market

Summary and Review of Basic Concepts

- Foreign exchange trading involves trading one country's currency for another. The need to exchange currencies arises from trading goods or investing across countries. The foreign exchange "market" refers to the activity of big commercial banks in international financial centers such as New York and London.

- The exchange rate is the price of one currency in terms of another. The spot market refers to immediate transactions (although technically they can take up to 2 days to clear).

- While currencies are often quoted at a single price, the price at which the currency is actually bought is a bit lower and the selling price is a bit higher. The difference between the two is the spread and constitutes the trader's profit. The spread will be larger if the currency is not frequently traded, or if the trader perceives the transaction to be risky.

- Nearly instant communication around the world ensures that exchange rates are virtually the same in all financial markets at any point in time. Differences between exchange rates means profitable, risk-free arbitrage can occur by buying a currency in one market and simultaneously selling it in another. The equality of cross rates is similarly ensured by triangular arbitrage.

- Forward exchange rates allow individuals to lock into an exchange rate now for a future transaction. By contracting now to buy or sell currency in the future, individuals are insulated from costly currency depreciations (or profitable currency appreciations). In other words, the risks of holding foreign exchange assets and liabilities can be balanced or hedged.

- If a currency's forward exchange rate is greater than the spot rate, it is said to sell at a forward premium. If the forward rate is less than the spot rate, it is said to sell at a forward discount.

- Rather than use forward exchange contracts, commercial banks often arrange currency swaps that combine spot and forward transactions in one deal. They borrow (loan) a currency now and agree to repay it (be repaid) at a future date at a certain exchange rate.

- Individual speculators or firms involved in international trade who wish to balance the risks of their currency exposure can choose to trade in a futures market. Futures contracts involve a specific amount of currency to be delivered at a specific maturity date.

111

- Futures markets require individuals to maintain minimum deposit balances, called margin requirements, with their brokers. That is, suppose a margin account of $2000 is established with a contract. As the exchange rates fluctuate daily, so will the potential profits or losses involved in the futures contract. If a trader's margin falls below the minimum, he will be asked to provide the broker with additional cash.

- Futures contracts involve daily cash flow settlements while forward contracts do not.

- Individuals or firms often purchase foreign currency options, which provide the right to buy or sell a given amount of currency at a fixed exchange rate on or before the maturity date (an "American" option; "European" options can only be exercised at maturity). A call option gives the right to buy currency, and a put option gives the right to sell.

- In an option, the price at which the currency can be bought or sold is the striking price. An option is "in the money" if the striking price is less than the current spot rate for a call, or greater than the current spot rate for a put.

- An advantage of options over futures or forwards is greater flexibility. A futures or forward contract is an obligation to buy or sell at a set exchange rate. An option offers the right to buy or sell if desired in the future and is not an obligation.

- Since exchange rates affect the prices of goods and services traded internationally, central banks may want to intervene in the foreign exchange market. Central banks can influence foreign exchange rates through policy announcements designed to change private market behavior, or by buying or selling either the domestic or foreign currency.

- Governments may restrict or even prohibit foreign currency transactions. As a result, illegal markets in foreign exchange, known as black markets, often develop to satisfy the demand. When these illegal markets exist openly or with implicit approval, they are referred to as parallel markets.

Appendix 13.1

- While the bilateral exchange rate provides useful information, a broader, global measure of a currency's value over time is sometimes more useful. Exchange rate indexes measure the average value of a currency relative to groups of other currencies.

- The index is usually weighted by the importance of each currency to international trade.

Define and/or Explain

exchange rate

spread

spot market

cross rate

depreciate

appreciate

forward exchange market

forward premium

forward discount

currency swap

hedging

margin

call

put

striking price (exercise price)

black market

parallel market

Multiple Choice

1. The difference between the buying and selling prices of a currency is called the

a. forward exchange rate.
b. spread.
c. spot market.
d. interest rate.

2.   Exchange rates are the same in different markets at the same time because

a.   all foreign exchange markets are linked to a central market administrator.
b.   each currency is traded in just one market.
c.   arbitrage will instantly eliminate market variations.
d.   of the existence of the forward market.

3.   Citibank's spread on the Cambodian riel will be larger than its spread on yen because

a.   trade in the riel is thinner.
b.   trade in the riel is riskier.
c.   neither of the above.
d.   both of the above.

4.   When a currency's forward exchange rate is greater than the spot rate

a.   it is selling at a forward premium.
b.   no one will buy the currency in the forward market.
c.   it is selling at a discount.
d.   arbitrage will eliminate the differential.

5.   If the exchange rate for German marks in U.S. dollars is US$/DM = .5591, then DM/US$ =

a.   1.7886
b.   1.9544
c.   0.8792
d.   1.2769

6.   If the exchange rate for the Australian dollar is US$/A$ = .7833 and the exchange rate for the Hong Kong dollar is US$/HK$ = .1280, then the Hong Kong-Australian dollar exchange rate (or how many HK$s does it take to buy one A$), HK$/A$ equals

a.   1.2767
b.   7.8133
c.   6.1195
d.   9.9738

7.   Suppose you are the First National Bank of Erehwon, and you have FF1,000,000 in your vault you will need to use in 60 days. Furthermore, you need ¥104,000 for the next 60 days. You arrange to loan your FF to the Hong Kong & Shanghai Bank for 60 days in exchange for ¥104,000 now, and reverse the transaction at the end of 60 days. You have just arranged

a.   to purchase a currency option.
b.   a currency swap.
c.   a futures contract.
d.   something completely illegal.

8.   You are purchasing a put option on Japanese Yen with a striking price of $.006992/¥. The Yen is now trading at $.006974/¥ on the spot market. Your option is

a.   a currency swap.
b.   above your initial margin.
c.   in the money.
d.   something completely illegal.

9.   You are the treasurer for an import-export company, and your firm has agreed to pay FF1,000,000 for equipment in 180 days. In addition, you have signed a contract to sell this equipment to a Singapore firm in 180 days for S$320,000. You are risk averse and want to hedge. You will

a.   buy the francs forward 180 days and simultaneously sell Singapore dollars forward 180 days.
b.   exchange the currencies on the spot market when they are due in 180 days.
c.   sell the francs forward 180 days and simultaneously buy Singapore dollars forward 180 days.
d.   buy an option for dollars.

10.   A central bank can influence foreign exchange rates in the following ways (may be more than one correct answer)

a.   announcing it will support its currency at a given exchange rate.
b.   announcing a non-interventionist policy.
c.   buying its currency on the market.
d.   selling its stock of foreign exchange on the market.

True or False?

T F   1.   European options can only be exercised at maturity.

T F   2.   You might not receive your currency until 2 days after your spot market transaction.

T F   3.   Parallel markets only deal in forward exchange rates.

T F   4.   Futures contracts require daily cash flow settlements.

T F   5.   Futures or forward contracts are more flexible than options.

T F   6.   A contract in the futures market involves a specific amount of currency to be delivered at a specific maturity date.

T F   7.   Swaps combine spot and forward transactions in a single deal.

T F   8.   The parallel market for foreign exchange in the United States is very large.

T F   9.   There will be no black market for U.S. dollars in a country where there are no restrictions on currency transactions.

T F   10.   The foreign exchange market operates only in New York and London.

Chapter 14

Prices and Exchange Rates:
Purchasing Power Parity

Summary and Review of Basic Concepts

- In previous chapters we saw how different prices for currencies in different markets leads to arbitrage, and how this arbitrage results in equal prices in all markets. We would similarly expect arbitrage to lead to equal prices for goods in different countries. In fact, there are reasons why some goods prices might be more similar across countries than others.

- One explanation for why exchange rates change over time is that exchange rates should adjust to offset differing inflation rates between countries. This relationship between prices and exchange rates is known as purchasing power parity.

- Absolute purchasing power parity (PPP) indicates that the exchange rate between any two currencies is equal to the ratio of their price indices, or $E = P/P^F$. Under these circumstances, the exchange rate is a nominal magnitude, and is dependent on prices.

- One problem with this formulation is that various national price indices must be comparable in terms of the goods and services covered.

- This relationship can be rewritten, $P = EP^F$ to show the relationship called the law of one price, meaning goods will sell for the same price worldwide.

- There are impediments to the equalization of goods prices, however, including differentiated products and costly information. The more homogeneous goods are, the more the law of one price should be expected to hold.

- In the relation $E = P/P^F$, there are reasons not to expect the ratio of price indices to hold, such as transportation costs and the inclusion of non-traded goods in the index basket.

- In addition to nominal changes in prices, relative price changes also occur, meaning some prices do not move together. Changes in relative prices can result in deviations from absolute PPP as the exchange rate changes even though the price indices are constant. The relative price effect leads to an appreciation of the currency where consumption of the good increasing in price is heaviest.

- A less restrictive statement on the relationship between prices and exchange rates is contained in relative purchasing power parity, $E = P - P^F$, where the percentage change in the exchange rate is equal to the inflation differential between the domestic and foreign country. (Note: For information on how this formula was derived, see the footnote on page 8 of the text.) If absolute PPP does not hold, relative PPP still may.

- Real events causing relative price movements are often random and short run in nature. Over time, relative price changes will decrease in importance compared to inflation rates, so that in the long run inflation differentials will dominate exchange rate movements.

- Economists have found that PPP holds better in two particular circumstances:
    - In countries with high levels of inflation, changes in exchange rates are highly correlated with inflation differentials because the enormous magnitude of inflation overwhelms the relative price effects. In lower inflation countries the relative price effects can dominate exchange rate movements and lead to deviations from PPP.
    - PPP holds better over a longer time frame since this allows for more inflation and random relative price effects become relatively unimportant.

- In general, economists have found that real relative price shifts can have important effects in the short run, but the random nature of the relative price changes over time minimizes the important of these unrelated events.

- Deviations from PPP might occur for a variety of reasons:
    - The law of one price would not apply to differentiated products, or products that are not traded internationally.
    - Prices may differ due to shipping costs or tariffs.
    - Relative price changes may result from economic events such as changing tastes, bad weather or government policy.
    - Since consumers in different countries consume different goods, price indices are not directly comparable internationally, thus leading to deviations from PPP even if the law of one price held for individual goods.

- There is also evidence that PPP does not hold well for many internationally traded goods. It should be noted that inflation differentials do not cause exchange rate changes. In other words, PPP is not a theory of exchange rate determination.

- Prices and the exchange rate are both endogenous variables that will change with changes in exogenous variables like the weather. Deviations in PPP will occur if prices and exchange rates change at different speeds.

- If commodity prices are not as flexible as financial asset prices, then deviations in PPP will result. In fact, exchange rates vary throughout the day as the demand and supply of foreign exchange varies, while goods prices are much slower to adjust. This is another reason why PPP holds better in the long run than in the short run.

- Periods with important economic news will be periods where PPP deviations are large, as price adjustments lag behind the exchange rate. These are also likely to be periods involving relative price changes as well, compounding PPP deviations.

- Substantial lags between order and delivery times may also result in deviations from PPP. Evaluations of PPP use current exchange rates applied to today's goods, even though the goods prices may have been set in the past.

- In sum, deviations from PPP have three basic sources:
  - the existence of factors that suggest permanent deviations (shipping costs and tariffs);
  - factors that would produce temporary deviations (differential speed of adjustment between financial asset markets and goods markets, or relative price changes);
  - factors that cause the appearance of deviations where none actually exist (comparing current exchange rates with prices set in the past, or using national price indices when countries consume different baskets of goods).

- For any pair of countries, when one price index P^F is expected to rise faster than P, yet the exchange rate does not fall by the amount suggested by the lower P/P^F, then the domestic currency is said the be undervalued or the foreign currency is overvalued.

- Since PPP does not hold well for any pair of countries in the short run with moderate inflation, currencies must always appear overvalued or undervalued in some sense. This is unimportant. It becomes important when this deviation persists and has macroeconomic consequences.

- Developing countries sometimes complain that their currencies are overvalued against the currencies of the developed countries. If PPP should apply only to internationally traded goods, then it can be shown that lower labor productivity in developing countries can contribute to the appearance of overvalued currencies.

- If the price indices used to calculate PPP include non-traded goods that incorporate low wages (from low-productivity labor), and exchange rates are determined by traded goods prices only, then price indices can vary substantially while exchange rates are constant.

- Over time, the currency of the lower productivity developing country will tend to appear overvalued, as the foreign exchange value of the developing country money will not depreciate to the extent called for by the change in average price levels.

120

Define and/or Explain

nominal

law of one price

relative price change

random

endogenous

exogenous

shock

"news"

spurious

Multiple Choice

1.   Arbitrage can be used in

a.   foreign exchange markets.
b.   goods markets.
c.   both of the above.
d.   none of the above.

2.   The law of one price

a.   is included in WTO rules.
b.   states that like goods will sell for the same equivalent price worldwide.
c.   makes arbitrage illegal.
d.   never holds.

3.   Purchasing power parity means

a.   exchange rates are the same in different foreign exchange markets at any given time.
b.   interest rates will be the same across countries at any given time.
c.   exchange rates will adjust to offset differing inflation rates between countries.
d.   the law of one price will never hold.

4.   In the relation $E = P/P^F$, P and P^F represent

a.   the inflation rates in the two countries.
b.   the prices for different goods in the two countries.
c.   the prices for two random consumption baskets.
d.   the domestic and foreign price levels.

5.   Absolute purchasing power parity implies

a. $E = P/P^F$.
b. $E = P - P^F$.
c.   consumption bundles differ between countries.
d.   goods sell for different prices between countries.

6.	In the relation $E = P/P^F$, reasons not to expect this ratio to hold include

a.	non-traded goods in the index baskets.
b.	transportation costs.
c.	costly information.
d.	both (a.) and (b.)
e.	(a.), (b.) and (c.)
f.	none of the above

7.	Suppose the French inflation rate this next year will be 4%, and British inflation will be 6%. The current exchange rate is FF/£ = 4.000. If relative PPP holds, we should expect next year's FF/£ exchange rate to be

a.	3.9216
b.	4.0800
c.	4.1600
d.	4.2400

8.	Relative price changes

a.	determine exchange rate movements in the long run.
b.	can change the exchange rate without changing the price levels.
c.	are eliminated by arbitrage.
d.	are always more significant than inflation.

9.	Choose the false answer. Relative price changes

a.	between traded and non-traded goods never occur
b.	become less important over the long run
c.	are less important with high rates of inflation
d.	can produce discrepancies from PPP

10.	It costs FF120 to have your car's oil changed in France. In Switzerland, it costs SF40 to have your car's oil changed. The exchange rate is FF3.5/SF1. This is an example of

a.	purchasing power parity.
b.	the law of one price.
c.	an opportunity for arbitrage.
d.	none of the above.

11.   Deviations from PPP may arise from all of the following except

a.   differentiated goods
b.   transportation costs or tariffs
c.   price indices composed only of traded goods
d.   fixed contract prices

True or False?

T F   1.   PPP rarely holds in cases of hyperinflation.

T F   2.   If the percentage change in the exchange rate is equal to the inflation differential between two countries, then relative PPP holds.

T F   3.   In general, inflation has little effect on exchange rates.

T F   4.   Developing countries' currencies often tend to be undervalued because of lower labor productivity.

T F   5.   PPP holds better in the long run than in the short run.

T F   6.   PPP will never hold when non-traded goods are included in the index.

T F   7.   If the exchange rate is equal to the ratio of the price indices, absolute PPP holds.

T F   8.   The law of one price applies to non-traded goods because of arbitrage.

T F   9.   Goods prices tend to adjust more quickly than exchange rates.

T F   10.   The more homogeneous goods are, the more we expect the law of one price to hold.

Matching

____ 1.   These two factors can result in permanent deviations from PPP.
____ 2.

____ 3.   These two factors can result in temporary deviations from PPP.
____ 4.

___ 5.   These two factors can cause the appearance of deviations from PPP even
___ 6.   though none really exist.

a.   price indices composed of different baskets of goods
b.   relative price changes
c.   tariffs
d.   financial asset prices adjust more quickly than goods prices
e.   shipping costs
f.   using the current exchange rate to evaluate previously determined prices

Chapter 15

Exchange Rates, Interest Rates, and Interest Parity

Summary and Review of Basic Concepts

- This chapter examines the relationship between interest rates and exchange rates. Interest rates are the return to holding interest-bearing financial assets. In the previous chapter, it was pointed out that financial asset prices (i.e. the exchange rate) tend to adjust more quickly to new information than goods prices. Like exchange rates, interest rates adjust quickly to new information.

- As individuals seek ways to profit in international asset markets, interest arbitrage will bring about an interest parity relationship.

- A U.S. investor deciding between investing in New York or in London must consider several things:
  - the interest rates, i$ and i£;
  - the spot exchange rate; and
  - the future exchange rate for the maturity date

- If the investor did not lock in a future exchange rate now, the unknown future spot exchange rate would make the investment risky. The investor can eliminate the uncertainty over the future dollar value of the investment by covering the investment with a forward exchange contract.

- Arbitrage between the two investment opportunities results in a covered interest parity condition:

$$(1 + i\$) = (1 + i\£)F/E \quad \text{or} \quad \frac{1 + i\$}{1 + i\£} = \frac{F}{E}$$

- The interest rate parity equation can be approximated by:

$$i\$ - i\£ = \frac{F - E}{E}$$

127

- If the forward exchange rates were not consistent with the respective interest rates, then arbitragers could profit by immediately changing currency in the spot market, investing it and locking in the (profitable) forward exchange rate. These actions in the market would increase the spot rate and lower the forward rate, bringing the forward premium into line with the interest differential.

- The effective return on an asset is given by the interest rate plus the expected change in the exchange rate. Suppose you used only the spot market with your investment. Suppose further that you receive 8% interest, i£, on your investment after one year. But when you go to change your pounds back into dollars, you find that the pound has appreciated against the dollar by 2% during the last year. This means your pounds buy 2% more dollars than they did before, and you have an effective return of 10%.

- Forward exchange rates incorporate expectations about the future spot exchange rate. If the forward exchange rate is equal to the expected future spot rate, then the forward premium is also the expected change in the exchange rate. In this case, uncovered interest parity is said to hold.

- Careful study of the data indicate that small deviations from interest rate parity do occur:

- Deviations may exist that are equal or smaller than the transactions costs, or else may be due to differential taxation, government controls, and political risk.

- The real interest rate reflects the nominal interest rate with an adjustment for inflation. Generally, the nominal rate of interest will tend to incorporate inflation expectations. The relationship between inflation and interest rates is given by the Fisher equation: $i = r + \pi$, where i is the nominal interest rate, r is the real interest rate, and π is the expected rate of inflation.

- If the real rate of interest is the same internationally, then the Fisher equation can be combined with the interest parity equation to obtain:

$$i\$ - i£ = \pi\$ - \pi£ = (F - E)/E$$

where nominal interest rates differ solely by differences in expected inflation.

- Real interest rates are equalized across countries when the Fisher equation, interest rate parity, and relative PPP all hold.

- If governments "peg" exchange rates at fixed levels through buying and selling foreign exchange to maintain the fixed rate, the domestic and foreign currency interest rates must adjust to parity levels.

- The structure of interest rates existing on investment opportunities over time is known as the term structure of interest rates. Interest rates can have a rising, flat or falling term structure. There are several theories explaining the term structure of interest rates.

  - Expectations: the long-term interest rate tends to equal the average of short-term rates expected over the holding period.

  - Liquidity premium: long-term instruments must incorporate a risk premium since investors prefer short-term investments.

  - Preferred habitat: there exist separate markets for short- and long-term assets, with interest rates determined by conditions in each market.

- Under conditions of freely flowing capital, the term structures in different currencies infer expected exchange rate changes, even if forward exchange markets for those currencies don't exist.

- If the term structure lines for two countries are:
  - parallel, then exchange rate changes are expected to be constant;
  - diverging, then the high-interest-rate currency is expected to depreciate at an increasing rate over time;
  - converging, then the high-interest-rate currency is expected to depreciate at a declining rate relative to the low-interest-rate currency.

Appendix 15.1

- Taxes can affect investment decisions also. If ty is the tax rate on income, and tk is the tax rate on capital gains, then equating the after-tax domestic return with after-tax foreign return yields

$$i\$(1 - ty) = i£(1 - ty) + (1 - tk)(1 + i£)[(F - E)/E].$$

- Rearranging, we have the after-tax interest parity equation

$$\frac{F - E}{E} = \frac{i\$ - i£}{1 + i£} \frac{1 - ty}{1 - tk}$$

- When ty and tk are not equal, the tax effect can become important. If capital gains are taxed at a rate lower than income, then there would be a greater incentive to invest in countries with a large forward premium since foreign exchange gains are taxed at the lower, capital gains rate. In other words, there will be a greater return to a dollar of foreign exchange gain than there will be to a dollar of interest.

Define and/or Explain

covered return

interest rate parity (covered)

effective return

interest rate parity (uncovered)

nominal interest rate

real interest rate

Fisher equation

term structure of interest rates

Multiple Choice

Consider the general relationship between interest rates and exchange rates for the United States and country X:

$$\frac{1 + i_{US}}{1 + i_X} = \frac{F}{E}$$

1. If the forward exchange rate is greater than the spot rate, then we know

a. the U.S. interest rate is lower than the foreign interest rate.
b. the U.S. interest rate is higher than the foreign interest rate.
c. the interest rates are the same.
d. no information on the interest rates is available.

Questions 2. through 8. refer to the table below.

Currency	$/unit
Canada-spot	.8574
90-day fwd	.8493
Japan-spot	.0068
90-day fwd	.0070
German-spot	.5591
90-day fwd	.5594

2. Which currency sells at a forward discount?

a. Canada
b. Japan
c. Germany
d. Japan and Germany

3. Japan's interest rate is _____ the U.S. interest rate.

a. higher than
b. lower than
c. the same as

4. Germany's interest rate is _____ the Canadian interest rate.

a. higher than
b. lower than
c. the same as

5.   Suppose the nominal 90-day U.S. interest rate is 1.875%, then Canada's nominal 90-day interest rate is approximately

a.   3.4%
b.   11.9%
c.   1.74%
d.   5.65%

6.   If the nominal annual U.S. interest rate is 7.5%, and U.S. inflation is 3.5%, then the real interest rate in the United States is

a.   11.5%
b.   7.5%
c.   4%
d.   3.5%

7.   If we assume the Fisher equation, interest rate parity, and relative purchasing power parity all hold, then according to the information above, the real interest rate in Japan is

a.   8%
b.   6%
c.   4%
d.   2%

8.   Suppose you invest today in 1-year Canadian bonds yielding 11.2%, and do not buy dollars forward to cover the transaction. One year from today you exchange your Canadian for U.S. dollars at a spot rate of US$.8746/Canadian dollar. The effective return on your investment is

a.   13.2%
b.   9.2%
c.   2%
d.   11.2%

9.   The real interest rate adjusts the nominal interest rate to account for

a.   exchange rate changes.
b.   covered interest arbitrage.
c.   the effective return.
d.   inflation.

10. If two governments permanently fix their exchange rates by agreeing to buy and/or sell foreign exchange to maintain the fixed rates, then

a. the interest rates in the two countries will differ.
b. the interest rates in the two countries must adjust to similar levels.
c. the nominal interest rate must also be the real interest rate.
d. purchasing power parity cannot hold.

11. The term structure of interest rates

a. examines the structure of interest rates on investment opportunities over time.
b. examines the effect of purchasing power parity on interest rates.
c. focuses on 90-day interest rates between two countries.
d. always rises.

12. The term structure of interest rates can be explained by all of the following except

a. long-term rates are the average of the short-term rates.
b. tax rates vary on short-term and long-term assets, so the long-term investments must offer a tax premium.
c. interest rates are determined independently in the short-term and long-term asset markets.
d. since investors prefer short-term investments, long-term assets must incorporate a risk premium.

13. If capital can flow into and out of markets freely, then the term structures in different currencies reflect

a. tax differentials.
b. inflation.
c. expected exchange rate changes.
d. the Fisher equation.

Appendix 15.1

14. If capital gains are taxed at a lower rate than interest income, then

a. international investment decisions will not be affected.
b. the high-interest-rate currency will depreciate.
c. inflation will make up the difference.
d. there will be a greater incentive to invest in countries with a large forward premium.

15. Suppose you pay 20% income tax, ty, and 10% capital gains tax, tk. You are deciding whether to invest your money for 90 days in either Japan or Germany for the same effective return, under the following conditions:

	$/unit
German-spot	.5484
90-day fwd	.5594
Japan-spot	.0068
90-day fwd	.0070

Your most profitable investment will be in

a. Germany
b. Japan

True or False?

T F 1. Exchange rate arbitrage equates exchange rates just as covered interest arbitrage equalizes interest rates worldwide.

T F 2. Covered interest arbitrage results in an interest parity relationship.

T F 3. Covering investments with a forward exchange contract reduces their exchange risk.

T F 4. Interest arbitrage generally equates the forward premium with the interest differential.

T F 5. The effective return on an asset is the interest rate minus expected inflation.

T F 6. Data have shown that there are never even minor deviations from interest rate parity.

T F 7. The Fisher equation describes the relationship between inflation, nominal and real interest rates.

T F 8. The differences between forward exchange rates and future spot exchange rates is known as the term structure of interest rates.

T F 9. If the term structure lines for two countries are converging, then the high-interest-rate currency is expected to depreciate at an increasing rate over time.

T F 10. Some economists believe the long-term interest rate tends to equal the average of short-term rates expected over the holding period.

134

T F   11.   In general, the term structures in different currencies reflect expected exchange rate changes.

T F   12.   If two investments in different countries have the same effective return, taxes will have no impact on the investment decision.

Chapter 16

Foreign Exchange Risk, Forecasting, and International Investment

Summary and Review of Basic Concepts

- Foreign exchange risk arises from uncertainty regarding the future. This chapter concerns international investment and capital flows, and the effect exchange risk has on them.

- A firm is exposed to foreign exchange risk in several ways:
  - translation exposure is the difference between foreign-currency-denominated assets and foreign-currency denominated liabilities;
  - transaction exposure results from the uncertain value of a foreign-currency-denominated transaction to be completed at some future date;
  - economic exposure is the risk to the value of the firm to changes in exchange rates. This is the most important type of risk to the firm.

- Translation exposure occurs when a foreign-currency-denominated balance sheet is translated in to the parent company's home currency. International accounting standards require foreign-currency denominated assets and liabilities to be translated at current exchange rates. When the currency used to denominate the foreign subsidiary's statement is depreciating relative to the dollar (the home currency), then the owner's equity will fall.

- Transaction exposure occurs when a firm commits itself to a future transaction without covering it through a forward transaction, thereby exposing it to exchange risk.

- Economic exposure is the vulnerability of future cash flows and hence the current value of the firm to changes in exchange rates.

- Although foreign exchange risk can be hedged by using the forward market and usually managed very carefully, recall that risk-taking can be profitable, as well. Managing cash flows, receivables and payables is a daily activity in multinational firms.

- If the forward rate differs from the expected future spot rate, then there is a risk premium incorporated into the forward rate. The risk premium induces others to absorb the risk in holding that currency.

- Individuals are generally more willing to accept riskier portfolios or assets if they are compensated with a higher return.

- From the interest parity relationship, we can see how the effective return differential is equal to the percentage difference between the forward and expected future spot exchange rate:

$$i - \frac{E*_{t+1} - E_t}{E_t} - i^F = \frac{F - E*_{t+1}}{E_t}$$

- The presence of a positive risk premium makes the forward rate a biased predictor of the future spot rate. Specifically, the forward rate overpredicts the future price of the currency to allow the risk premium.

- A market is efficient if prices reflect all available information. In the foreign exchange market this means that spot and forward exchange rates will adjust quickly to new information.

- Studies of foreign exchange market efficiency have had mixed results, largely because of the difficulty of testing efficiency ex post. If a researcher can find a forecasting rule that is a better predictor of past spot rates than was the forward rate, it (a) may not be useful for future speculation, and (b) since it wasn't known in the past, doesn't rule out market efficiency.

- While a smaller forecasting error is preferable to a larger error, it is more important to be on the correct side of a forward rate than to have a small forecast error. The closer you are to the actual rate from the correct side, the more money you can make. If you cross beyond the actual rate (on the wrong side), you lose money.

- Evidence that some forecasting advisory services can consistently beat the forward rate is not necessarily evidence of a lack of market efficiency. If the difference represents transaction costs or the price of the service, no abnormal profits can be made. If the difference represents a risk premium, the returns would be a normal compensation for risk bearing.

- International investment is only partially motivated by interest differentials between countries. Even freely flowing capital will not equalize interest rates worldwide since risk differs among assets. Even with identical interest rates, however, capital will flow due to the desire to diversify portfolios.

- Investors interested in the future value of their portfolio will want to reduce the variation of the future value of the portfolio. The variance of the return on a portfolio can be statistically represented by

$$var(R_p) = a^2var(R_A) + b^2var(R_B) + 2abcov(R_A,R_B)$$

where var is the variance, or degree to which the variable fluctuates around its mean, and cov is the covariance, or the degree to which the two assets move together.

- The lower risk achieved by diversification leads investors to hold many different assets, including assets from different countries.

- Variance that can be eliminated through portfolio diversification is called nonsystematic risk. Systematic risk is due to events that are experienced jointly by all firms, such as the business cycle.

- Some of what would be considered systematic risk in a strictly domestic portfolio becomes nonsystematic risk when foreign investments are included as well. Therefore, investors can realize additional gains by diversifying across countries.

- Direct foreign investment can also be seen as an aspect of return subject to risk considerations, as motivates all firm decisions. But if markets were perfectly competitive, then the domestic firm could just as well buy foreign securities to transfer capital abroad rather than actually establish a foreign operating unit.

- A literature has developed to offer more specific motives for DFI that typically explain the incentive in terms of a market imperfection. Firms locate abroad due to:
  - technology transfer of superior skills, knowledge or information that allow the foreign subsidiary to earn a higher return;
  - economies of scale permitted by multiple plants;
  - a desire to appropriate the foreign market before competitors can enter.

- Direct investment was more important than bank lending as a source of funds in developing countries prior to the oil shocks of 1973-74. Through the late 1970s, bank lending grew more important with the recycling of petrodollars. Bank lending was preferred by developing countries because it allowed greater flexibility in the use of funds and was more acceptable politically.

- As bank lending has been curtailed, direct investment has become an important source of funds again. Direct investment may contribute more to economic development than bank loans because:
  - more funds go to actual investment in productive resources rather than to consumption spending;
  - direct investment may involve new technologies and productive expertise;
  - losses are sustained by the foreign firm and not the domestic government.

139

- When the risk of investment in a country rises sharply or the expected return falls for either political or financial reasons, large outflows of investment funds occur via huge capital account deficits, described as capital flight.

- Estimates of the magnitude of capital flight over 1977-87 period of the international debt crisis, suggest that it was equivalent to a sizeable portion of the total debt incurred through that time. Capital outflow means that fewer resources are available at home to service the debt (especially dollar-denominated), and more borrowing is required. This is also often associated with a loss of international reserves and greater pressure for devaluation of the domestic currency.

Define and/or Explain

exchange risk exposure

risk premium

risk aversion

efficient market

short position

long position

diversified portfolios

variance

covariance

systematic risk

nonsystematic risk

capital flight

Multiple Choice

1. Translation exposure is

a. the difference between foreign-currency-denominated assets and foreign-currency-denominated liabilities.
b. a foreign-currency-denominated transaction to be completed at a future date.
c. the sensitivity of the value of the firm to changes in exchange rates.
d. none of the above

2. All of the following involve foreign exchange risk for a French multinational firm except

a. The firm pays all employees worldwide an annual bonus equivalent to 1000 French francs in local currency.
b. The firm must incorporate the balance sheet of its Brazilian subsidiary into its own for the annual earnings statement.
c. The firm agrees to deliver a product to a customer in Hong Kong in 60 days and covers the transaction in the forward market.
d. The firm owes a supplier in Argentina A50,000 due in 90 days.

3. This is an appropriate hedging strategy against foreign exchange risk.

a. Minimize accounts payable in a weak currency.
b. Minimize bank deposits in the strong currency.
c. Specify payables and receivables in the strong currency.
d. Shorten credit terms for customers paying in a weak currency.

4.   Foreign exchange risk may be hedged or eliminated by

a.   utilizing the forward or futures market.
b.   invoicing in the foreign (weaker) currency.
c.   speeding payments denominated in the currency expected to depreciate.
d.   speeding collection of currencies expected to depreciate.
e.   both (a.) and (d.)
f.   both (b.) and (c.)

5.   Suppose the 6-month interest rate in the US is 7 percent and 3 percent in Japan. The spot exchange rate is $.0083. You would expect the forward rate to be

a. $.0057
b. $.0086
c. $.0085
d. $.0060

6.   Given the data in question 5, suppose the forward rate is $.0085, but you expect the dollar to appreciate against the yen by 2% over the next 6 months. You think the spot rate (E^*_{t+1}) will be

a. $.0056
b. $.0081
c. $.0085
d. $.0059

7.   Given the information in questions 5 and 6, the foreign exchange risk premium on the yen is

a.   .096
b.   .048
c.   .021
d.   .030

8.   With these expectations and market conditions in questions 5-7, your effective return from holding a Japanese bond will be

a.   .054
b.   .073
c.   .078
d.   .059

9.	A forward exchange rate contains an exchange risk premium

a.	when the effective return differential is zero.
b.	when the forward and expected future spot exchange rates differ.
c.	when interest rates differ.
d.	when the spot rate is expected to change.

10.	An efficient market is one where

a.	the spread is zero.
b.	all available information is reflected in prices.
c.	prices don't change.
d.	a well-informed investor can make consistent profits without undertaking substantial exchange risks.

11.	Tests of foreign exchange market efficiency

a.	always show the foreign exchange market to be efficient.
b.	show the foreign exchange market to be consistently inefficient.
c.	show mixed results.

12.	If interest rates in two countries were identical and the exchange rate was constant

a.	there would still be incentives for international capital flows.
b.	there would be a large risk premium.
c.	there would be no incentive for international capital flows to occur.
d.	risk would be identical in the two countries.

Questions 13-16 are based on the following:
Suppose you want to invest equally in two projects but have three possible investment opportunities, each offering the same expected return. They have the following characteristics:

	variance	covariance
project A	.5	cov(A,B)= .5
project B	.7	cov(A,C)= .25
project C	.2	cov(B,C)= -.4

13.	The variance of the return on a portfolio split equally between projects A and B will be

a.	.40
b.	.55
c.	-.30
d.	0.0

14. The variance of the return on a portfolio split equally between projects A and C will be

a. .35
b. .62
c. .26
d. .30

15. The variance of the return on a portfolio split equally between projects B and C will be

a. .42
b. -.37
c. .01
d. .025

16. You choose to invest in

a. projects A and B.
b. projects A and C.
c. projects B and C.

17. Direct foreign investment (DFI) can be explained by all of the following except

a. It is less risky to transfer capital abroad by investing in productive resources than it is to buy foreign securities.
b. A firm might possess skills or knowledge that allows it to earn a higher return.
c. Firms wish to diversify their assets in order to maximize return subject to risk considerations.
d. Firms wish to prevent foreign competitors from entering the market.

18. Choose the false answer. Direct investment may contribute more to economic development than loans because

a. Losses must be sustained by the foreign firm and not the domestic government.
b. DFI receives a lower rate of return than commercial loans.
c. Funds go into productive resources rather than to consumption spending.
d. Direct investment often involves new technology and expertise.

True or False?

T F 1. Exposure to foreign exchange risk can be profitable.

T F 2. The presence of a risk premium makes the forward rate a biased predictor of the future spot rate.

T F   3.   Since some forecasting services predict exchange rates better than the forward rates, we know the foreign exchange market is inefficient.

T F   4.   In forecasting exchange rates, it is more important to have a small forecast error than to be on the correct side of the forward rate.

T F   5.   Owners of firms are most concerned with transaction exposure.

T F   6.   When the currency used to denominate a foreign subsidiary's statement varies relative to the parent company's standard currency, the owners' equity will absorb the losses or gains from translation exposure.

T F   7.   You own a US firm with foreign subsidiaries. You bought a machine for your factory in Mexico in 1985. When you report the value of the machine on the parent firm's financial statements, you value it according to the 1985 exchange rate.

T F   8.   International capital flows are solely a function of interest rate differentials.

T F   9.   We should not expect interest rates to be equalized worldwide since risk differs among assets.

T F   10.   Portfolio diversification eliminates systematic risk.

Chapter 17

Basic Theories of the Balance of Payments

Summary and Review of Basic Concepts

Elasticities Approach to the Balance of Trade

- The elasticities approach to the balance of trade is concerned with how changing relative prices of domestic and foreign goods will change the balance of trade.

- When the relative price of a good changes, the quantity demanded of that good will change. How much the quantity demanded changes in response to the relative price change is determined by the elasticity of demand for that good.

- The elasticities approach analyzes how devaluations will affect the balance of trade, depending on the elasticities of supply and demand for foreign exchange and/or foreign goods.

- When supply or demand is elastic, it means that the quantity supplied or demanded will be relatively responsive to the change in price.

- The elasticities of demand and supply can be written:

$$\epsilon_d = |\%\Delta Q_d / \%\Delta P|$$

$$\epsilon_s = \%\Delta Q_s / \%\Delta P$$

- When demand is elastic (greater than one), the quantity sold changes by a greater percentage than the price. For example, if the price of a good decreases, sales increase by a greater percentage and total revenue increases. The same relationship holds true for the elasticity of supply.

- Consider the importance of the elasticity of demand and supply for foreign exchange. From an initial equilibrium, there is an increase in the demand for foreign exchange. The possible responses are:
  - with freely floating exchange rates, the price of the foreign currency (the exchange rate) will rise;

- if the central bank pegs the exchange rate at the original rate, it must allow reserves to flow out (providing the appropriate supply of foreign exchange);
- foreign exchange controls or quotas can be imposed to restrict the demand and supply of foreign exchange;
- tariffs or quotas on goods can be imposed to maintin the original demand and supply of foreign exchange.

- The elasticities approach is a theory of the balance of trade, and can only be a theory of the balance of payments in a world without capital flows.

- Suppose the increase in demand for foreign exchange is met with a central bank devaluation (the price of foreign exchange is increased). The effect of this policy on the trade balance depends on the elasticities of supply and demand. From an initial trade deficit, if demand for imports is inelastic so that the price of imports increases but the quantity of imports demanded changes little, the trade deficit could worsen.

- This worsening trade balance following a devaluation is called the "J curve." Over time, elasticities increase so that the balance of trade improves.

- The behavior of the trade balance immediately following a devaluation can be determined by the currency-denomination of existing contracts that remain to be completed. The results could range from immediate improvement, to no change, to immediate deterioration.

- Pass-through analysis considers the ability of prices to adjust in the short run. If goods prices do not adjust immediately to devaluations, then spending patterns will not change and there will be no trade balance effect. Depending upon the elasticities of supply and demand for imports and exports, the trade balance could immediately improve, remain constant, or deteriorate.

- Evidence suggests that the effects of devaluation appear to differ across countries and time so that no strong generalizations are possible.

- One reason for the variety of responses in trade balances to exchange rate movements is that producers differ in the degree to which they adjust profit margins on exports following an exchange rate change. Japanese exporters are known to "price to market" by lowering the yen price of their products to counter the effect of a yen appreciation. U.S. exporters are more likely to allow full pass through.

Absorption Approach to the Balance of Trade

- This approach emphasizes how domestic spending on domestic goods changes relative to domestic output. The balance of trade is viewed as the difference between what the economy produces and what it consumes.

- Recall from basic principles $Y = C+I+G+(X-IM)$. Define absorption as $A = C+I+G$, substitute and rearrange to yield

$$Y - A = X - IM$$

- If domestic production (Y) exceeds absorption, the rest will be exported. Moreover, the excess of domestic demand over domestic production will be met through imports.

- At full employment, all resources are utilized and exports can only be increased by decreasing domestic absorption. Devaluation will boost exports and result only in inflation as domestic prices are bid up.

- With unemployment, output is not at its maximum level and exports could increase without cutting into domestic absorption. Devaluation will increase exports and output without inflation.

- The absorption approach provides a theory of the balance of trade and can only be viewed as a theory of the balance of payments in a world without capital flows.

Monetary Approach to the Balance of Payments

- This approach incorporates financial assets as well as merchandise into the theory of the balance of payments and emphasizes the monetary aspects of the balance of payments.

- The basic premise of the MABP is that any balance of payments disequilibrium is based on a monetary disequilibrium, or a difference between the amount of money people want to hold and the amount supplied by the monetary authorities. The analysis accordingly emphasizes the determinants of money demand and supply.

- The MABP describes completely a world with fixed exchange rates (or a gold standard). In a world with flexible exchange rates, the monetary approach to the exchange rate (MAER) must be incorporated. The flow of money or exchange rate changes substitute as adjustment mechanisms.

- Consider a small open economy. The model contains equations for the (a) demand for money, (b) supply of money, and (c) relationship between prices and the exchange rate:

$$L = kPY$$

$$M = R + D$$

$$P = EP^F$$

Substituting and evaluating in terms of percentage changes, we have:

$$\hat{R} - \hat{E} = \hat{P}^F + \hat{Y} - \hat{D}$$

- With fixed exchange rates, money supply adjusts to money demand through international flows of money (reserves) via balance of payments imbalances. With flexible exchange rates, money demand will be adjusted to a money supply set by the central bank via exchange rate changes.

- The monetary approach to the balance of payments assumes exchange rates are fixed and that reserves change in response to the remaining variables. The monetary approach to the exchange rate assumes reserves are constant, so that the exchange rate absorbs changes in the variables as individuals try to increase their money balances.

- The managed float contains the attributes of both a fixed and floating exchange rate regime since changing supply and demand will affect exchange rates, but the actions of the central bank also allow international reserves to change.

- In this framework, the assumption of purchasing power parity means that the central bank must make a policy choice between an exchange rate or a domestic price level. Maintaining a fixed exchange rate implies the domestic price level will correspond to the rest of the world.

- There are two views of how PPP operates in the short run, and they imply different adjustment mechanisms to changes in the world economy.

- PPP holds strictly, even in the short run, and foreign price changes are immediately reflected in domestic prices and the demand/supply of money.

- Prices adjust slowly through the balance of payments effects on the money supply.

- These two views differ principally with regard to timing. The first case of rapid adjustment emphasizes the role of financial assets and capital flows. The second approach emphasizes the role of goods markets in international adjustment.

- The monetary approach to the balance of payments has these policy implications:

  - Balance of payments (BoP) disequilibria are monetary phenomena. Countries run long-term trade deficits by relying on money supply growth to finance government spending.
  - BoP disequilibria are transitory. With fixed exchange rates, the country will eventually run out of reserves by supporting a deficit.
  - BoP disequilibria can be handled with domestic monetary policy rather than exchange rate adjustments.

150

- The BoP can be improved by an increase in domestic income via an increase in money demand, if not offset by an increase in domestic credit.

Appendix 17.1

- The appendix explores the implications of a devaluation for the trade balance given inelastic demands for imports and exports. (It complements the previous discussion of the J curve.)

- If the foreign demand for U.S. exports is inelastic, this indicates that the foreign exchange supply curve to the United States will be negatively sloped.

- If the demand curve has a steeper slope than the supply curve (if the U.S. import demand is more inelastic than demand for our exports), then a devaluation will increase the excess demand for foreign exchange, and the market is unstable.

- The Marshall-Lerner condition indicates that a devaluation will improve the U.S. trade balance and provide a stable foreign exchange market if the elasticity of demand for U.S. imports plus the elasticity of demand for U.S. exports is greater than one. If the sum of the two elasticities is less than one, the foreign exchange market will be unstable and the devaluation will cause the trade balance to fall.

Define and/or Explain

relative price

elasticity

J-curve effects

currency contract period

pass-through

pricing to market

absorption

adjustment mechanism

base money

domestic credit

international reserves

small open economy

Multiple Choice

1. The elasticities approach to the balance of trade

a. focuses on the effects of changing relative prices of domestic and foreign goods on the balance of trade.
b. is only applicable with freely floating exchange rates.
c. is based on an analysis of the absolute prices of a country's exports in world markets.
d. indicates that the demand elasticity for exports is always inelastic.

2. When demand is elastic,

a. ϵ_d is greater than zero.
b. sales decrease when the price decreases.
c. sales increase by proportionately more than the price decreases.
d. supply must be inelastic.

3. "Indonesian coffee exports have boomed over the past year, but with prices at a decade low, total revenues equal last year's." This implies the elasticity of demand for Indonesian coffee exports is

a. inelastic (less than one)
b. approximately one
c. elastic (greater than one)

4. From an initial equilibrium, an increase in demand for foreign exchange can be met by all of the following except

a. allowing the price of foreign currency to fall.
b. allowing reserves to flow out with a fixed exchange rate.
c. having the central bank increase the supply of foreign exchange and maintain the exchange rate.
d. maintaining the exchange rate and rationing foreign exchange

5. From an initial equilibrium, a decrease in demand for foreign exchange will most likely result in

a. an increase in the price of foreign currency.
b. accumulating reserves under a fixed exchange rate.
c. import quotas.
d. foreign exchange rationing.

6.	The "J curve"

a.	only occurs under fixed exchange rates.
b.	occurs when a currency is appreciated.
c.	represents an initial worsening of the balance of trade with devaluation.
d.	always accompanies a devaluation.

7.	Pass through

a.	occurs only under fixed exchenge rates.
b.	will continue indefinitely.
c.	will not occur in the J curve.
d.	describes the ability of prices to adjust in the short run.

8.	Under the absorption approach,

a.	absorption refers to private sector purchases (C+I).
b.	the excess of domestic demand over domestic production will be met through imports.
c.	output greater than absorption results in unemployment.
d.	both (a.) and (c.)

9.	Under the absorption approach, a devaluation will

a.	always result in inflation.
b.	tend to increase imports.
c.	have different effects depending on whether there are unemployed resources in the economy.
d.	not have any impact.

10.	The monetary approach to the balance of payments

a.	focuses on the importance of the current account balance.
b.	views exchange rate variation as the sole adjustment mechanism.
c.	highlights the role of financial assets in balance of payments adjustment.
d.	implies that the price level and exchange rate can both be determined by the central bank.

11.	In the monetary approach, purchasing power parity (PPP)

a.	is assumed to hold.
b.	is irrelevant.
c.	is important only with fixed exchange rates.
d.	imply balance of payments disequilibria are not necessarily monetary phenomena.

True or False?

T F 1. A decreased demand for foreign exchange will often result in a devaluation (an increased price for foreign exchange).

T F 2. The currency contract period can contribute to the J-curve phenomena with a devaluation.

T F 3. A country with an inelastic demand for imports and an elasticity of demand for its exports equal to one will experience a falling trade balance with a devaluation.

T F 4. The sharp decline in the value of the U.S. dollar against most other currencies in 1986, and the growing trade deficit that followed could be considered evidence of a J-curve.

T F 5. Evidence shows that a devaluation always has the same result on the trade balance.

T F 6. Japanese exporters are noted for their reluctance to lower the yen price of their products in response to an appreciation of the yen.

T F 7. A decrease in the exchange rate is equivalent to an appreciation of the domestic currency.

T F 8. In the monetary approach to the balance of payments, when income or foreign prices increase, individuals try to increase their money balances and we should observe a decrease in the value of the domestic currency.

T F 9. Under the absorption approach an increase in exports will have the same result under conditions of full factor employment or unemployment.

T F 10. The flow of reserves or exchange rate changes are substitute adjustment mechanisms in the MABP.

T F 11. With a fixed exchange rate in the MABP, foreign inflation will bring about U.S. inflation.

T F 12. Argentina relies on the rapid growth of the money supply to finance government spending. The MABP tells us the government should also be able to maintain a fixed exchange rate.

T F 13. The Marshall-Lerner condition indicates that a devaluation will improve a trade deficit if the country's elasticity of demand for imports and the elasticity of demand for that country's exports sum to less than one.

156

Chapter 18

Exchange Rate Theories

Summary and Review of Basic Concepts

- Prior to the 1970s, economists saw trade flows as the primary determinants of exchange rates, due in part to the fact that governments maintained tight restrictions on international flows of financial capital.

- With financial liberalization, however, the volume of trade in financial assets now dwarfs trade in goods and services. Accordingly, current theories emphasize the role of the exchange rate as one of many prices in the worldwide market for financial assets.

Asset Approach

- In modern models, the exchange rate is viewed as adjusting to equilibrate international trade in financial assets.

- One implication of the asset approach is that since the prices of financial assets change rapidly, exchange rates should be much more variable than goods prices.

- The asset approach typically assumes perfect capital mobility. In such a world, covered interest arbitrage will ensure covered interest rate parity:

$$(i - i_f)/(1+i_f) = (F-E)/E$$

where i is the domestic interest rate and i_f is the foreign interest rate. The relationship will hold continuously, and spot and forward exchange rates and interest rates will adjust instantly to changing conditions.

- Among asset approach models, there are two basic types: the monetary approach (as in the MABP), and the portfolio balance approach.

- In the monetary approach (MA), the exchange rate for any two currencies is determined by relative money demand and money supply between the two countries. Relative supplies of domestic and foreign bonds are unimportant.

- The portfolio balance (PB) approach allows relative bond supplies and demands as well as relative money market conditions to determine the exchange rate.

- The MA models assume domestic and foreign bonds to be perfect substitutes, while PB models assume imperfect substitutability.

- The PB approach assumes that assets are imperfect substitutes because investors perceive foreign exchange risk to be attached to foreign-currency-denominated bonds. With imperfect substitutability, demanders have preferences for distributing their portfolio over different countries' assets.

- In general, PB models have risk premia in the forward exchange rate that are a function of relative asset supplies. Since the forward market incorporates risk premia, this implies that uncovered interest rate parity will not hold.

- The BP approach can be seen by modifying the MA equation found in the last chapter to include the percentage change in the supply for foreign bonds relative to the supply of domestic bonds:

$$-\hat{E} = \hat{P}^F + \hat{Y} - \hat{D} + \hat{B}^F - \hat{B}$$

- An increase in the growth rate of foreign bond supplies causes the domestic currency to appreciate at a faster rate. An increase in domestic bond supplies' growth rate causes the domestic currency to depreciate at a faster rate.

- Empirical evidence is not clear on this because of central bank activities aimed at insulating the domestic money supply from international events, such as sterilization.

- Sterilization refers to central banks offsetting international reserve flows in order to follow an independent monetary policy.

- For example, if there are barriers to capital mobility that lead to delayed arbitrage, the monetary authorities may be able to determine the money supply in the short run without having reserve flows offset the monetary authorities' goals.

- If sterilization occurs, then the causality implied in the basic MA equation is no longer true.

- Changes in domestic credit lead to changes in reserves, but with sterilization, changes in reserves could then affect domestic credit.

- The PB model permits sterilized intervention to alter the exchange rate, even though money supplies are ultimately unchanged. In the MA, the relative bond supplies are deleted from the equation, and the only way that a sterilized intervention could change the exchange rate would be if money demand changed and affected income or prices.

- It is possible to integrate trade flows into a model where the exchange rate is determined by desired and actual financial asset flows, so that the role of trade flows in exchange rate determination may be consistent with the modern asset approach to exchange rates.

- For example, if the exchange rate adjusts so that the stocks of domestic and foreign money are willingly held, then a country with a trade surplus will be accumulating foreign currency. As holdings of foreign money increase relative to domestic money, their relative value will fall, or the foreign currency will depreciate.

- Expectations regarding the future balance of trade and its implied currency holdings can affect the expected future spot rate, and future expected values of a currency can have an immediate impact on the current spot rate.

Overshooting Exchange Rates

- Since exchange rates adjust more rapidly than goods prices, the different speeds of adjustment can lead to a situation where it appears that the spot exchange rate moves too much for a given disturbance. This is called overshooting exchange rates.

- The key elements in analyzing this phenomenon are the money supply, prices, interest rates, and the exchange rate. Consider first money demand that depends positively on income ($a>0$) and negatively on the interest rate ($b < 0$):

$$L = aY + bi$$

- Consider also that in the short run following an increase in the money supply, both income and the price level are relatively constant.

- With an increase in the money supply and the price level constant in the short run, the interest rate must drop in order to equate money demand with the now-higher money supply.

- This drop in the interest rate has a direct and immediate impact on the exchange rate through the interest rate parity relationship.

- We know prices will adjust in the longer run and an exchange rate consistent with PPP will evolve. But the initial effect will be a drop in the interest rate adequate to absorb the entire shock to the money supply and consequently, an increase in the spot exchange rate above the long run equilibrium rate.

- Only as prices gradually adjust will the interest rate and exchange rate move to their long run equilibrium levels.

Currency Substitution

- One of the advantages of flexible exchange rates is that countries become independent in their ability to formulate domestic monetary policy. This domestic policy independence is reduced, however, if there is an international demand for currencies.

- As long as everyone believes that the exchange value of two currencies will never change, then money demanders will be indifferent between holding the two currencies. If this is no longer true, then currency substitution becomes an additional source of exchange rate variability. It could cause a currency to depreciate even more than initially called for by an inflation differential.

- Suppose two currencies are held in a region (say, near a border). If one currency becomes associated with a higher inflation rate than the other, citizens will want to get rid of the high-inflation currency in favor of the low-inflation currency. Although we would normally expect the low-inflation currency to appreciate on PPP grounds, the shift in currency demand will accentuate the depreciation of the high-inflation currency.

- Regions with a high degree of currency substitution may therefore benefit from international coordination of monetary policy. A high degree of substitutability may lead to a currency union with fixed exchange rates and coordinated monetary policy

- It is important to remember that the world is characterized by unforseen shocks and surprises that affect interest rates, prices and exchange rates. Predicting future spot rates becomes more difficult when we know the exchange rate will be determined by unpredictable events.

- Even with a good knowledge of the determinants of exchange rates, actual exchange rates will always prove to be difficult to forecast in a world filled with surprises.

Define and/or Explain

perfect capital mobility

portfolio balance approach

sterilized intervention

currency union

Multiple Choice

1. Economists have traditionally viewed trade flows as the primary determinants of exchange rates. Current theories of exchange rate determination focus on

a. macroeconomic coordination.
b. demand and supply of financial assets.
c. sterilization.
d. currency unions.

2. There are two basic types of exchange rate determination models that focus on flows of financial assets, (choose two)

a. the monetary approach.
b. the overshooting hypothesis.
c. the "news" approach.
d. the portfolio balance approach.
e. the sterilization approach.
f. the covered interest parity approach.

3. An implication of the asset approach is that

a. since financial asset prices change rapidly, exchange rates should vary more than goods prices.
b. since the law of one price holds, goods prices should change as rapidly as the exchange rate.
c. covered interest parity will rarely hold if there is perfect capital mobility.
d. goods prices will be largely unaffected by exchange rate changes in the long run.

4. The basic difference between the monetary approach (MA) and the portfolio balance approach (PB) is

a. the PB approach incorporates only domestic stocks and bonds into the model.
b. the monetary approach looks at flows of cash, but not other financial assets.
c. the MA models assume domestic and foreign bonds to be perfect substitutes, while PB models assume imperfect substitutability.
d. unlike the MA approach, the PB approach implies individuals have no incentive to distribute their portfolio over various currency assets

161

5. From an initial equilibrium, suppose the supply of foreign bonds rises relative to domestic bonds. In the PB model, as the supply of foreign bonds rises, an increased risk premium will be incorporated into the price of the foreign bonds which will cause the domestic currency to

a. depreciate.
b. appreciate.
c. to maintain the same value relative to the foreign currency.

6. Empirical evidence comparing the MA and PB approaches shows

a. the PB approach clearly explains market behavior better than the MA approach.
b. the MA approach is better than the PB approach.
c. they perform equally well.
d. it is difficult to demonstrate that either is a superior predictor, partly because of market intervention activities and news.

7. Sterilization refers to

a. central bank activities to offset the impact of international reserve flows on the money supply.
b. maximizing the risk premium on holding foreign bonds.
c. eliminating foreign bonds from the domestic market.
d. central bank activities that cause domestic and foreign bonds to become perfect substitutes.

8. Central banks might want to undertake sterilization activities in order to

a. improve capital mobility.
b. follow an independent monetary policy.
c. protect domestic money holders.
d. offset foreign exchange risk.

9. In the modern asset market approach to exchange rates, trade flows

a. are insignificant and have no impact in the models.
b. partially offset the flow of financial assets.
c. respond to exchange rate changes, but cannot affect the exchange rate.
d. are consistent with financial asset flows in determining exchange rates.

10. Currency substitution

a. increases a central bank's ability to carry out independent monetary policy.
b. occurs when there is no international demand for the currency.
c. can result in increased volatility in domestic exchange rates.
d. occurs only with fixed exchange rates.

11. Currency unions

a. can be useful in regions where currency substitution is common.
b. occur when a group of countries jointly issues a single, common currency.
c. require fixed exchange rates but allow independent monetary policies.
d. result in higher inflation.

12. Overshooting exchange rates

a. show that the asset market approach is rarely able to predict exchange rates.
b. occur when the spot rate appears to move too much in response to an economic disturbance.
c. results from imperfect domestic knowledge about foreign bonds.
d. is a long run phenomenon.

13. Overshooting exchange rates occur because

a. it takes time for foreigners to fully understand news in the domestic market.
b. the prices of goods adjust more rapidly than financial asset prices.
c. money demanders often act irrationally in the short run.
d. sluggish price changes in the goods market cause the interest rate to absorb the full impact of the shock in the short run.

True or False?

T F 1. Exchange rates are primarily determined by trade in goods and services.

T F 2. There is no evidence to show that prices of goods or financial assets behave differently.

T F 3. The exchange rate is one example of a price for a financial asset.

T F 4. The monetary approach assumes individuals diversify their portfolios across countries.

T F 5. Imperfect substitutability of financial assets is characteristic of the portfolio balance approach.

T F   6.   Sterilization efforts are successful only if there are no barriers to capital mobility and capital flows immediately in response to market changes.

T F   7.   In a portfolio balance framework, a country's trade deficit will lead to increased holdings of foreign currencies and an appreciation of the domestic currency.

T F   8.   Money demand is generally a positive function of income.

T F   9.   An overshooting exchange rate occurs because goods prices adjust relatively slowly compared to interest rates.

T F   10.   Currency substitution is more likely between adjacent countries.

Chapter 19

Alternative International Monetary Standards

Summary and Review of Basic Concepts

- Discussions of modern international monetary history usually begin with the late nineteenth century and can be divided into: the gold standard, the inter-war years, the post-World War II gold exchange standard, and the transition to floating exchange rates.

- Under the gold standard, currencies are valued in terms of a gold equivalent, or mint parity price. Since each currency is defined in terms of its gold value, all currencies are linked in a system of fixed exchange rates.

- The maintenance of a gold standard requires a commitment from each participating country to buy and sell gold to anyone at the mint parity price.

- A currency that has a fixed value in gold, a commodity, is said to be on a commodity money standard. A commodity money standard must be based on a homogenous commodity that is easily storable, portable, divisible into standardized units, and is of relatively fixed supply.

- A money standard based on a commodity with relatively fixed supply will lead to long-run price stability. In the case of gold, national money supplies were constrained by the growth of the stock of gold.

- Under a gold standard, balance of payments disequilibria are easily remedied:
  - A country running a balance of payments deficit would experience net outflows of gold, reducing its money supply and hence, its prices.
  - A country running a balance of payments surplus would experience net inflows of gold, increasing its money supply and hence, its prices.
  - Falling prices in the deficit country would lead to increasing net exports, while rising prices in the surplus country would lead to decreasing net exports, eventually restoring balance of payments equilibrium.

- The gold standard effectively ended at the beginning of World War I with government manipulation of gold and foreign exchange transactions.

- Most of Europe experienced rapid inflation during the war and immediately following; hence pre-war parities no longer held and a restoration of the gold standard at the old exchange values was not possible. The United States, however, had experienced little inflation and returned to a gold standard by 1919 at the old parity.

- In spite of higher prices, in 1925 England also returned to a gold standard at pre-war parity. Consequently, the British money supply contracted as gold purchases soared, and by 1931 the pound was declared inconvertible.

- With British inconvertibility, the demand for gold was focused on the U.S. market. A "run" on U.S. gold at the end of 1931 resulted in a 15% drop in U.S. gold holdings. By 1933, the United States raised the official price of gold to $35 per ounce in order to halt the gold outflow.

- The depression years of the 1930s were characterized by international monetary warfare in the form of competitive devaluations. In order to increase GNP, governments attempted to manipulate net exports by controlling foreign exchange transactions. With the onset of World War II, foreign exchange controls were used to assist financing the war effort.

- An international post-war conference at Bretton Woods, New Hampshire in 1944 resulted in the creation of the "Bretton Woods Institutions," including the International Bank for Reconstruction and Development (IBRD, or World Bank), the International Monetary Fund (IMF), and the International Trade Organization (which evolved into the General Agreement on Tariffs and Trade, or GATT and has since become the World Trade Organization).

- As a result of this conference, participating countries agreed to fix the values of their currencies in gold (the par value). Since an ounce of gold was defined as being equal to US$35.00, all currencies were linked to the dollar and each other in a system of fixed exchange rates. Central banks were obligated to maintain parity (plus or minus one percent) by buying and/or selling their currencies on international markets.

- This system is sometimes called the adjustable peg system, or the gold exchange standard because the key currency, the dollar, could be converted into gold for official holders (such as central banks or treasuries). Moreover, countries with balance of payments problems were permitted to devalue their currencies via changes in the par value.

- The IMF was created to monitor the operation of the system and provide short-term loans to countries experiencing temporary balance of payments disequilibria. Successive loans are subject to increasingly strict conditionality aimed at restoring balance of payments equilibrium.

- In the 1960s, financing the war on poverty and the Vietnam war through expansionary monetary policy led to large foreign holdings of dollars. As central banks exchanged their dollar holdings for U.S. gold reserves, fears developed that the dollar would be devalued in terms of gold. This led to a higher demand for gold in private markets, as well, and a heavy gold outflow from the United States.

- The international economic powers uniformly maintained their unwillingness to realign currency values in the face of fundamental economic change throughout the 1960s. Pressure on the dollar finally culminated in suspension of U.S. gold sales (Nixon's "closing the gold window") in August 1971 and marked the end of fixed exchange rates.

- An international monetary conference was held in December 1971 at the Smithsonian Institute in Washington, D.C. The resulting Smithsonian Agreement moved the gold exchange value from US$35 to US$38 per ounce and revalued currencies of surplus countries. Further, central banks agreed to buy or sell their currencies to maintain their exchange rates within 2.25 percent of parity.

- The realignment in the Smithsonian Agreement provided a short-lived respite. Pressure in the system built until June 1972, when the British pound was allowed to float. By late 1972 and early 1973, currency speculators began selling massive amounts of U.S. dollars, leading to a further devaluation of the dollar in February 1973. By March 1973, all major currencies were floating.

- Although exchange rates since 1973 are described as a floating rate system, central banks often intervene to obtain desirable exchange rates. Some countries allow their currencies to float freely, while others maintain a fixed value (or peg) relative to a single currency, and others peg to a basket of currencies. Some countries choose the intermediate path between the float or the peg, known as the crawling peg.

- Opinion is mixed on the desirability of floating or fixed exchange rates:
  - flexible rates enable countries to follow independent macroeconomic policies;
  - differing inflation rates will result in varying exchange rates;
  - fixed rates impose international discipline on inflationary policies of countries, forcing governments to conform to the international standard;
  - flexible rates are subject to destabilizing speculation.

- Countries choose fixed or floating exchange rates depending upon several factors:
  - large countries tend to be less willing to subjugate domestic policy to maintain a fixed exchange rate;
  - more open economies tend to follow a pegged exchange rate, while more closed economies prefer a floating rate.

- Countries that trade largely with a single foreign country tend to peg their exchange rates to the foreign country's currency. Those with more diversified trading patterns might peg to a basket of currencies.

- The choice of an exchange rate system will also affect the stability of the economy. If the domestic policy-makers seek to minimize unexpected fluctuations in the domestic price level, they will choose the exchange rate system that best minimizes those fluctuations:
    - the greater are fluctuations in foreign tradable goods prices, the more likely the currency is to float in order to insulate the domestic economy from foreign price disturbances;
    - the greater the fluctuations in the domestic money supply, the more likely the currency will be pegged in order to reduce the domestic price impact of domestic money supply fluctuations.

- A currency area is an area where exchange rates are fixed within the area, while floating exchange rates exist against currencies outside the area. An optimum currency area is the best grouping in which to achieve an objective such as ease of adjustment to real or nominal shocks.

- One theory suggests that the optimum currency area is the region characterized by relatively costless mobility of the factors of production (labor and capital). Conversely, when factors are immobile so that equilibrium is maintained through changes in relative goods prices, there may be an advantage to maintaining flexible exchange rates.

- The European Monetary System (EMS) was established in 1979 to maintain exchange rate stability in Western Europe. The Exchange Rate Mechanism (ERM) required the central banks of member countries to intervene in currency markets to keep exchange rates within a 2.25 percent band.

- The ERM became difficult to operate when European capital flows were deregulated and member countries pursued dissimilar macroeconomic goals. Britain and Italy pulled out of the ERM in 1992 in the face of speculative selling of pounds and lira.

- The Maastricht Treaty of 1991 laid out specific steps for Europe to have a single currency by the end of the century.
    - removal of restrictions on European capital flows and greater coordination of monetary and fiscal policy
    - establishment of European Monetary Institute to prepare for a single monetary policy
    - the irrevocable fixing of exchange rates with the European Currency Unit becoming a circulating currency

- Target zones allow the exchange rate to fluctuate within a limited range around some central fixed value.

168

- Currency boards have been used in some countries to achieve a credible fixed exchange rate. A currency board is a government institution that exchanges domestic currency for foreign currency at a fixed exchange rate.

- Relatively few currencies serve the role of money in the international economy and are known as reserve currencies. As with any money, a reserve currency must serve as a unit of account, a medium of exchange, and a store of value.

- A reserve currency has an informational advantage over other currencies and is often used as an invoicing currency in international contracts.

- A reserve currency is so widely traded that it is often cheaper to move from one currency to, say, dollars, and then to another currency, than it is to move directly between the two non-dollar currencies: use of the reserve currency is more efficient.

- Stability of value, or certainty of future value, enhances a currency's role as a store of purchasing power.

- Although the U.S. dollar is not the only reserve currency, it is the dominant reserve currency. The share of foreign exchange reserves in U.S. dollars has been falling since the mid-1970s, with a rising share held in German marks and Japanese yen.

- Governments may resist a greater international role for their currencies as they find that international shifts in the demand for their monies may have repercussions on domestic monetary policy. For example, international capital flows of any given magnitude have a much smaller potential to disrupt U.S. markets than Japanese, German or Swiss markets.

- A composite currency is an artificial currency composed of an average of several real currencies. Examples include the SDR and the ECU.

- Many countries peg their exchanges rates to the SDR or other composite currencies. With trade diversified across countries, it may be advantageous to peg to an average of the trading partners' currencies. Bank deposits or bonds may be denominated in a composite currency as it is generally more stable than a single currency.

- The SDR is essentially a form of international reserve issued by the IMF to member countries. Since 1981, its value has been calculated as a weighted average of the value of five major currencies (U.S. dollar, German mark, French franc, Japanese yen, and UK pound).

- Although some business transactions are denominated in SDRs, the volume of these transactions is dwarfed by the volume denominated in single currencies such as the U.S. dollar. The very limited private use of the SDR denomination includes bonds, bank deposits, certificates of deposit, and infrequently, syndicated bank loans and financial contracts.

169

- The ECU was introduced by the European Monetary System in 1979 with the ultimate goal being its use in domestic economies in order to achieve a common European money. Its value is determined as a weighted average of the EU currencies. Like the SDR, there is no physical ECU currency; ECUs are accounting entries and serve as reserve assets of the EMS.

- Unlike SDRs, however, there has been growing use of ECUs over time to denominate private transactions. Bank deposits, syndicated loans, bond issues, travelers checks and even life insurance are increasingly denominated in ECUs.

- The ECU has been more readily accepted than the SDR for several reasons. First, since it excludes the U.S. dollar completely, it is a more effective hedge against the dollar. Second, the EMS commitment to stable exchange rates has made its exchange value very stable.

- Some countries maintain a system of multiple exchange rates. For example, there may be a fixed exchange rate for current account transactions, with a market-determined floating exchange rate for capital account transactions.

- Generally, multiple exchange rates harm the countries that impose them. Multiple exchange rates distort the domestic relative prices of traded goods, with consequent distortions in consumption, production and investment decisions. Individuals also devote vast (scarce) resources to finding ways to profit from the system. Such a system also requires costly administration.

Define and/or Explain

gold standard

commodity money standard

SDR

EMS

ERM

Maastricht Treaty

crawling peg

destabilizing speculation

seigniorage

ECU

target zone

currency board

Multiple Choice

1.   All of the following are true under a gold standard except

a.   each currency has a mint parity price.
b.   all monies are some form of gold coin for participating countries.
c.   fixed exchange rates prevail.
d.   all currencies are linked to each other through their prices in gold.

2.   In POW camps during the Vietnam War, cigarettes were used as money. This is an example of a

a.   commodity money standard.
b.   gold standard.
c.   gold exchange standard.
d.   Bretton Woods Institution.

3.   Under these circumstances, cigarettes met all of the requirements for money except that they might not be (choose the most likely)

a.   easily storable.
b.   portable.
c.   divisible into standard units.
d.   of relatively fixed supply.

4.   In a cigarette-based economy, which of the following circumstances will most likely result in long-run price stability?

a.   the quantity of cigarettes in the economy increases at a constant rate.
b.   the quantity of cigarettes in the economy decreases at a constant rate.
c.   the quantity of cigarettes in the economy remains relatively fixed.
d.   the quantity of cigarettes in the economy fluctuates randomly.

5.   Under a gold standard in a world where only goods flow internationally, a country running a current account deficit will experience a

a.   net inflow of gold and rising prices.
b.   net inflow of gold and declining prices.
c.   net outflow of gold and rising prices.
d.   net outflow of gold and declining prices.
e.   balance of payments equilibrium.

6.   Under a gold standard in a world where only goods flow internationally, a country running a current account surplus will experience a

a.   net inflow of gold and rising prices.
b.   net inflow of gold and declining prices.
c.   net outflow of gold and rising prices.
d.   net outflow of gold and declining prices.
e.   balance of payments equilibrium.

7.   Trading nations followed a gold standard

a.   in the late 19th century and up to the beginning of World War I.
b.   only during World War I and World War II.
c.   during the world-wide depression of the 1930s.
d.   during periods of inconvertibility.

8.   The Bretton Woods Conference

a.   established rules for freely floating exchange rates.
b.   enabled the United States to close the gold window.
c.   established the gold exchange standard, among other things.
d.   prompted a run on U.S. gold holdings.

9.   The par value

a.   refers to the value of a country's currency in terms of U.S. dollars after adjusting for differences in inflation.
b.   of a currency was fixed in terms of gold.
c.   is the value of a country's short-term loans from the IMF.
d.   was the value of a country's international reserves after World War II.

10.   The International Monetary Fund

a.   was responsible for all international gold reserves after World War II.
b.   financed the Marshall Plan.
c.   controlled all foreign exchange transactions world-wide.
d.   was created to ensure the smooth operation of the gold exchange standard.

11.   Fixed, or pegged exchange rates and convertibility

a.   essentially ended in the early 1970s when the United States was no longer willing to sell gold at the prevailing exchange rates.
b.   were eliminated with the Smithsonian Agreement.
c.   must now be maintained within 2.25 percent of parity.
d.   are strictly enforced by the IMF.

12. Since 1973, currency values

a. float freely according to demand and supply
b. are pegged to the value of a single currency
c. are pegged to a basket of currencies
d. follow a crawling peg through market intervention
e. all of the above

13. Flexible exchange rates

a. enable countries to follow independent macroeconomic policies.
b. allow inflation rates to vary across countries.
c. force governments to conform to international inflation standards.
d. enable destabilizing speculation.
e. both (a) and (c)
f. (a), (b) and (d)

14. Which country below would be most likely to peg its exchange rate to a basket of currencies?

a. Singapore
b. United States
c. Soviet Union
d. Liberia

15. An example of a currency area is

a. the SDR.
b. the EMS.
c. both (a) and (b)

16. As originally set out in 1979, the ERM required central banks to maintain bands of what size on the exchange rates of member countries?

a. 1 percent
b. 2.25 percent
c. 7.5 percent
d. 10 percent

17. Under the Maastricht Treaty, which of the following is not a requirement for a country to join the European monetary union?

a. The country's inflation rate must not be more than 1.5 percentage points above the average of the lowest three member country rates.
b. Its interest rates on long–term government bonds must not be more than 2 percentage points above the average of the three lowest inflation members.
c. Its trade balance must not be more than +3 percent or less than –3 percent of its GDP.
d. Its government budget deficit must not exceed 3 percent of its GDP.

18. A reserve currency must

a. have a fixed value in terms of gold.
b. be pegged to the U.S. dollar.
c. serve as a unit of account, a medium of exchange, and a store of value.
d. be easily storable, portable, divisible into standard units, and of relatively fixed supply.

19. An example of a composite currency is

a. the SDR.
b. the ECU.
c. both (a) and (b)

20. Financial instruments such as bank deposits or bonds might be denominated in a composite currency because

a. they have lower tax rates.
b. the composite currency is generally more stable than a single currency.
c. they earn higher interest rates.
d. the composite currency is pegged to the price of gold.

21. Multiple exchange rates

a. are illegal.
b. occur naturally for reserve currencies.
c. exist only for the SDR.
d. may be determined by government policy.

22.   Multiple exchange rates

a.   increase world welfare.
b.   harm only the countries that impose them.
c.   distort prices, trade, investment, and consumption.
d.   are costless.
e.   (b) and (c)

23.   A government institution that exchanges domestic currency for foreign currency is called a:

a.   monetary fund.
b.   exchange fixing reserve.
c.   currency board.
d.   EMS.

24.   A plot of the exchange rate (on the vertical axis) against "fundamentals" (on the horizontal axis) will follow an S-shaped path with:

a.   flexible exchange rates.
b.   a credible target zone.
c.   fixed exchange rates.
d.   a crawling peg.

True or False?

T F   1.   The competitive devaluations of the 1930s were intended to increase economic activity by stimulating net exports.

T F   2.   The IMF was created at the Bretton Woods Conference.

T F   3.   The SDR is pegged to the U.S. dollar.

T F   4.   The value of an ECU will increase as the value of the German mark decreases.

T F   5.   The IMF is an agency of the U.S. Government.

T F   6.   ECUs are used more commonly than SDRs to denominate financial assets.

T F   7.   The SDR is a better hedge against U.S. inflation than the ECU.

T F   8.   SDRs can be obtained at banks for spending overseas, just like pounds or yen.

T F   9.   The U.S. dollar is the dominant international reserve currency, but rising shares are held in German marks and Japanese yen.

T F   10. In all countries, economic stability is best assured by allowing exchange rates to float freely.

T F   11. Decontrol of European capital flows contributed to the breakdown of the ERM in 1992.

T F   12. A currency board provides credibility that the government will maintain the fixed exchange rate.

T F   13. Target zones lock the exchange rate into a fixed value permitting no fluctuation.

Chapter 20

International Banking, Debt, and Risk

Summary and Review of Basic Concepts

- The international market for deposits and loans is known as the Eurocurrency market. The provision of these services is often called offshore banking.

- Although the Eurodollar market originally referred to U.S. dollar-denominated banking activities carried out by European financial institutions, it now is understood to encompass transactions in any currency outside that currency's country-of-origin.

- Offshore banking activities have grown rapidly over the past several decades because of a lack of regulation which allows greater efficiency in providing banking services. This greater efficiency allows Eurobanks to offer a narrower spread than domestic banks.

- U.S. banks are subject to regulation by U.S. government agencies. Specifically, they must hold a fraction of their deposits in the form of noninterest-bearing reserves, are subject to interest rate controls, deposit insurance requirements, mandated credit allocations, and market restrictions. In contrast, Eurocurrency banking activities are largely unregulated.

- More stringent banking regulation increases the cost of banking services. Hence, the spread in offshore banks is generally smaller than in U.S. banks. The U.S. deposit rate provides an interest rate floor for the Eurodeposit rate, and the U.S. loan rate provide a ceiling for Euroloan rates.

- Eurodollar loan interest rates are usually quoted in terms of percentage points above the London Interbank Offer Rate, or LIBOR.

- While the domestic spread usually provides the constraints on the currency's external interest rates, this may not hold in the case of capital controls.

- Threats of confiscation or restrictions on private property rights could also lead to interest rate distortions. In general, risk contributes to the domestic spread exceeding the external spread.

- International Banking Facilities (IBFs) have been legal in the United States since 1981. Prior to that time, U.S. banks established branches in places like the Bahamas and the Cayman Islands where financial services are not regulated (hence the term "offshore" banking).

- The legalization of IBFs enables banks to offer two types of services: one for residents of the United States, and one for nonresidents and other IBFs. The second set of transactions are kept separate from the banks' other business because IBFs are not subject to reserve requirements, interest rate regulations, or Federal Deposit Insurance Corporation deposit insurance premiums.

- Because of the importance of interbank transactions, gross deposits at Eurobanks overstate the importance of these banks in intermediating funds between nonbank savers and nonbank borrowers. To measure the amount of credit extended through Eurobanks, we subtract interbank activity from total deposits.

- The existence of an active Eurocurrency market may have implications for domestic monetary practices.

- In countries without efficient money markets, access to a competitive Eurocurrency market may reduce the demand for domestic money as individuals can shift funds to the offshore market and obtain a competitive return.

- If international reserve flows are greater due to the international capital flows encouraged by Eurodollar market efficiency, then central banks must engage in larger and more frequent sterilization operations to achieve a given domestic money growth policy.

- Deposits in the Eurocurrency market are for fixed terms ranging from days to years, although most are for less than six months. Loans in this market can range up to ten years or more. The interest rate on a loan is quoted as a percentage over LIBOR and is usually adjusted every three months.

- When the OPEC nations raised the price of oil (always payable in U.S. dollars) in the 1970s, their massive balance of payments surpluses were usually deposited in Eurodollar accounts. These petrodollars were then loaned ("recycled") to developing countries.

- As the developed countries fell into recession in the early 1980s, the demand for the debtor-country exports fell as did the prices of their exports. At the same time, high and rising interest rates increased the cost of these loans. This squeeze turned into what is known as the "debt crisis" as many developing countries became unable to service the debt they had contracted.

- When countries are unable to make payments on their debt, they can default (just stop paying) or reschedule. Rescheduling means the terms of the loan are renegotiated--often capitalizing the unpaid interest, postponing and/or extending the repayment of principal and interest.

- Official debt (money borrowed from a government) can be rescheduled through the Paris Club. Before meeting with its creditors, however, a country must arrange a standby agreement with the IMF.

- Private or commercial debt can also be rescheduled through committees representing the commercial banks (sometimes called the London Club).

- Private debt of many countries can be bought or sold on a secondary market. Generally, commercial banks are willing to sell developing country debt when it is unlikely to be repaid on its original terms. The higher the probability of the debt not being repaid, the lower the value of the debt.

- Some debtor countries and banks carry out debt-equity swaps. In a swap, a private company buys a country's debt from a bank at a reduced price, and exchanges that debt instrument at the country's central bank for domestic currency that is then used to finance investment in the country.

- The IMF is involved in debtor-creditor activities in several ways. The IMF is a source of direct funding for some countries. Their most important role, however, is facilitating rescheduling.

- In order to reschedule with the Paris Club, a country must first negotiate a standby agreement with the IMF. In negotiating the standby, the debtor country must work with the IMF and agree to domestic policy changes that will enhance its long-term growth prospects and thus increase its ability to service its debt in the future. These IMF-required adjustment programs are known as IMF conditionality.

- The IMF is an international institution controlled by its member countries. IMF policy is determined by members' votes, which are allocated according to the size of a country's financial contribution (its quota) to the Fund. The United States has the most votes, with nearly 20 percent of the total. The United States, United Kingdom, Germany, France and Japan together control more than 40 percent of IMF votes.

- The lack of international courts to enforce international contracts, such as loans to foreign firms or governments, has led to an increasing emphasis on country risk analysis. Country risk refers to the overall political and financial situation in a country and the extent to which these conditions may affect the ability of a country to repay its debts.

- Political factors for evaluation include: splits between different language, ethnic, and religious groups that undermine stability; extreme nationalism and xenophobia that could lead to differential treatment of foreigners or nationalization of foreign holdings; unfavorable social conditions; social conflict evidenced by demonstrations, violence, and guerilla war; strength and organization of radical groups.

181

- Financial factors for evaluation include: level of external debt as a share of GNP or export earnings; international reserve holdings relative to imports; level and diversity of exports; real GNP growth.

Define and/or Explain

Eurocurrency market

LIBOR

IBFs

petrodollars

Paris Club

debt-equity swap

Multiple Choice

1.   The Eurocurrency market refers to

a.   deposits and loans of currencies outside issuing markets.
b.   European currency transactions in New York.
c.   domestic European financial markets.
d.   the European Monetary System.

2. Offshore banks must

a. hold a fraction of deposits in reserves.
b. conform to interest rate controls.
c. pay for deposit insurance.
d. follow credit allocation guidelines.
e. all of the above
f. none of the above

3. The extensive use of offshore banking markets

a. is illegal for U.S. citizens.
b. is a result of the tax-free status of interest earned in these accounts.
c. is due to their narrower spread.
d. is subject to IMF regulation.

4. LIBOR stands for

a. London International Bid-Offer Requirement.
b. Leveraged Interbank Overdraft Requirement.
c. London Interbank Offer Rate.
d. Liquid International Borrowings on Reserves.

5. International banking facilities in the United States

a. cannot operate legally.
b. are usually operated along-side normal banking activities.
c. are usually located in Florida.
d. are subject to the same regulations as any U.S. financial institution.

6. Petrodollars

a. were used by OPEC countries for official development assistance (ODA, or foreign aid).
b. were invested in OPEC industries.
c. were deposited in the International Monetary Fund.
d. were deposited in Eurodollar accounts in the 1970s and recycled to developing countries.

7. Official debt can be rescheduled through the

a. International Monetary Fund.
b. Paris Club.
c. London Club.
d. World Bank.

8.   When a country carries out a debt-equity swap,

a.   it buys back part of its commercial bank debt from a foreign company which invests the money locally.
b.   it sells a government enterprise to a foreign commercial bank in exchange for its bank debt.
c.   it allows a foreign commercial bank to operate tax-free in that country.
d.   it trades commercial debt for equity in export industries.

9.   The IMF is sometimes known as the "Rich Countries' Club" because

a.   only developed countries are members.
b.   only five industrialized countries control 42 percent of the votes.
c.   membership is very expensive.
d.   developing countries are members, but have no votes.

10.   Conditionality refers to

a.   higher interest costs that come with larger debt burdens.
b.   the terms under which countries become members of the International Monetary Fund.
c.   targeted investment for commercial loans.
d.   performance and policy requirements set by the IMF in order to obtain IMF loans.

True or False?

T F   1.   Communist countries are prohibited from holding Eurocurrency accounts.

T F   2.   Eurocurrency markets have no impact on domestic monetary policies.

T F   3   Eurobanks are essentially unregulated.

T F   4.   Euroloan rates are quoted as a percentage above or below the U.S. prime rate, and are fixed for the life of the loan.

T F   5.   In general, high risk leads to an external spread greater than the domestic spread.

T F   6.   The international banking system is dominated by U.S. and Japanese banks.

T F   7.   Interbank positions are the assets held in a bank's overseas offices.

T F   8.   IBFs in the United States are subject only to reserve requirements.

T F   9.   An active Eurocurrency market can require larger and more frequent sterilization operations by central banks.

T F   10.   Developing countries' expected interest payments can fluctuate because the interest rate on Euroloans is usually adjusted every three months.

Matching

___1. Very large loans are usually made by these.

___2. Rescheduling can

___3. Your country must generally agree to this before the IMF will loan you money.

___4. OPEC recycled these.

___5. This serves as the interest rate ceiling on Euroloans.

___6. This serves as the interest rate floor for the Eurodeposit rate.

___7. A commercial bank must evaluate this before lending.

___8. A country's membership contribution to the IMF is its

___9. The secondary market for developing country debt is

___10. This is required before you go to the Paris Club.

a.   U.S. deposit interest rate
b.   IMF standby arrangement
c.   conditionality
d.   petrodollars
e.   U.S. loan rate
f.   syndicates of Eurobanks
g.   extend the terms of repayment
h.   very thin
i.   quota
j.   country risk

Chapter 21

Open Economy Macroeconomic
Policy and Adjustment

Summary and Review of Basic Concepts

- Basic goals in the open economy are to achieve: internal balance, a steady growth of the domestic economy with a low unemployment rate, and external balance, a desired trade balance or level of international capital flows.

- The open economy differs from the closed economy in that policy-makers must consider the impact of policies on the balance of trade, capital flows and exchange rates in addition to employment and inflation.

- Major tools of macroeconomic policy are fiscal policy (government spending and taxation), and monetary policy (central bank control of the money supply).

- Macroeconomic equilibrium requires equilibrium in three major sectors of the economy:
    - goods market equilibrium, where the quantity of goods and services supplied is equal to the quantity demanded, summarized in the IS curve;
    - money market equilibrium, where the quantity of money supplied is equal to the quantity demanded, summarized in the LM curve;
    - balance of payments equilibrium, where the current account deficit (surplus) is equal to the capital account surplus (deficit) so the official settlements balance equals zero, summarized in the BP curve.

- Graphically, macroeconomic equilibrium is achieved where the IS-LM-BP lines intersect.

Deriving the IS Curve

- Equilibrium in the goods market requires finding the combinations of i and Y that yield S+T+IM = I+G+X.

- Consider first the relationship between S+T+IM, I+G+X and income. Both savings and desired imports increase as income grows, yielding an upward sloping S+T+IM curve. Since investment depends largely on the interest rate and not income, and exports and government spending are considered exogenous, they can be represented by a horizontal line determined by the interest rate. The intersection of these two lines is the point where S+T+IM = I+G+X.

186

- Now let the interest rate vary. Investment will increase when the cost of investing, the interest rate, declines. Thus the horizontal I+G+X line will shift up or down as the interest rate changes. A higher interest rate results in lower investment and a lower equilibrium level of output. A lower interest rate results in higher investment and a higher equilibrium output level.

- As a result, the IS curve is downward sloping. Furthermore, this IS curve is drawn holding the domestic price level and the exchange rate constant.

Deriving the LM Curve

- Equilibrium in the money market requires finding the combinations of i and Y at which money demand equals money supply.

- Consider first the relationship between money demand and the interest rate. The interest rate is the opportunity cost of holding money. Therefore, the higher the interest rate, the smaller the amount of desired money holdings. This yields a downward sloping money demand curve. Money supply is exogenously determined. Equilibrium occurs at the intersection of the two lines, where money demand equals money supply.

- Now let income vary. Since money demand increases at higher levels of income, the money demand line will shift up as income increases, resulting in a higher equilibrium value of the interest rate.

- This yields an upward sloping LM curve, drawn for a given money supply. Increases in the money supply shift the LM curve outward.

Deriving the BP Curve

- The BP curve gives combinations of i and Y that yield balance of payments equilibrium, where the current account surplus (deficit) equals the capital account deficit (surplus). Consider first the relationship between the current account, capital account and income. As income increases desired imports increase and the current account falls, yielding a downward sloping current account line. The capital account is drawn as a horizontal line since it is independent of income.

- When the interest rate increases, domestic financial assets become more attractive, capital flows in, and the capital account deficit falls.

- Equilibrium in the economy requires that the goods market, the money market and the balance of payments all be in equilibrium. The occurs when the IS, LM, and BP curves intersect at a common interest rate and level of income.

Fixed Exchange Rates

- Begin with the assumptions that domestic and foreign financial assets are perfect substitutes, and capital is perfectly mobile. Under these circumstances, the domestic and foreign interest rates must be equal, and the BP curve is a horizontal line at the domestic (and foreign) interest rate.

- Increasing the money supply will cause the LM curve to shift out, resulting in a higher income and lower interest rate. But the lower interest rate prompts a capital outflow and downward pressure on the exchange rate. The central bank must sell reserves to buy domestic currency, thus decreasing the domestic money supply and shifting the LM curve back to restore initial equilibrium.

- An increase in government spending will shift the IS curve to the right, with a higher interest rate and level of income. Foreign capital flows in, putting upward pressure on the exchange rate. The central bank must buy foreign exchange with domestic currency, thus increasing the money supply and shifting LM out to the right. Equilibrium now occurs at the original interest rate but at a higher level of income.

Floating Exchange Rates

- The principle difference in this analysis (often called the Mundell-Fleming model) is that with floating exchange rates, the central bank is not obliged to intervene in the foreign exchange market to support any given exchange rate. Since the assumption of perfect asset substitutability is maintained, the BP curve will still be horizontal with domestic and foreign interest rates equal. However, equilibrium in the balance of payments will require the exchange rate to change when economic conditions change.

- Depreciation of the domestic currency will make domestic goods relatively cheaper and stimulate domestic exports, shifting the IS curve to the right.

- An increase in the money supply shifts the LM curve to the right, with a lower interest rate and higher income. But the lower interest rate prompts capital to flow out, and causes the domestic currency to depreciate. This shifts the IS curve to the right, eventually leading to equilibrium at the original interest rate but a higher level of income.

- An expansionary fiscal policy will shift the IS curve to the right, with a higher domestic interest rate and level of income. The higher interest rate prompts a capital inflow, and the value of the currency increases. Currency appreciation shifts the IS curve back to the left, eventually leading to equilibrium at the original interest rate and level of income.

- When expansionary fiscal policy has no effect on income, complete crowding out has occurred.

- Crowding out could be minimized if governments coordinated policies. If all governments simultaneous stimulated their economies, the world interest rate would rise and the pressure for exchange rate change and net export adjustment would fall (in other words, the BP curve would move upward). Monetary policy-induced changes could similarly be lessened.

- Some economists argue in favor of international policy coordination in order to stabilize exchange rates. They argue that reduced exchange rate volatility would reduce the destabilizing effect of undervalued or overvalued currencies.

- Other economists view exchange rate changes as the result of real economic shocks such as changes in tastes or technology. Under these conditions, exchange rates are always in equilibrium and government policy is best aimed at lower inflation and a stable domestic economy.

The Open Economy Multiplier

- Assuming that saving and import demand are each proportional to income and that the interest rate is fixed, equilibrium national income can be expressed as $Y = (I + G + X - T)/(s + m)$, where s is the marginal propensity to save and m is the marginal propensity to spend on imports. This equation shows how equilibrium income depends on investment, government spending, export demand, and taxes.

- The term $1/(s + m)$ is the national income multiplier. The multiplier must be larger than one, since some fraction of an additional dollar's worth of income will be spent on domestically-produced goods, rather than saved or spent on imports.

- If demand for U.S. goods rises by $10 billion, say because of an increase in demand for exports, national income will go up by more than $10 billion. This is the multiplier at work. The rise in export demand directly raises income by $10 billion, as additional resources of that value must be employed in export industries to meet the new demand. Some of this extra income will then be spent on other domestic goods, contributing to additional employment and income in the economy. If this process is followed to its logical conclusion, the total incremental change in national income can be represented by $\$10/(s + m)$.

Define and/or Explain

internal balance

external balance

189

IS curve

LM curve

BP curve

Mundell-Fleming model

crowding out

open economy multiplier

Multiple Choice

1. A country maintains an internal balance when

a. domestic investment is greater than foreign investment.
b. the current account equals zero.
c. the domestic interest rate and the unemployment rate are equal.
d. steady growth and low unemployment are achieved.

2. A country maintains an external balance when

a. U.S. investment overseas is equal to foreign investment in the United States.
b. a desired trade balance or level of capital flows is achieved.
c. the balance of trade is zero.
d. there is zero net capital outflow.

3.   All of the following are tools of macroeconomic policy except

a.   government spending.
b.   taxes.
c.   a government's tariff policy.
d.   the central bank's control of the money supply.

4.   Government spending and taxes are examples of a government's

a.   fiscal policy.
b.   foreign policy.
c.   monetary policy.
d.   trade policy.

5.   Macroeconomic equilibrium in an open economy requires

a.   goods market equilibrium.
b.   money market equilibrium.
c.   current account balance equal to zero.
d.   balance of payments equilibrium.
e.   all of the above
f.   (a), (b) and (d)

6.   Balance of payments equilibrium means

a.   the balance of trade equals zero.
b.   the current account balance equals zero.
c.   the capital account balance equals zero.
d.   the current account balance is exactly offset by the capital account balance so the official
      settlements balance equals zero.

7.   Consider the open economy shown in Figure 1
      at the right. Internal balance in this
      economy is achieved at

a.   only point a
b.   only point b
c.   points b or c
d.   only point d

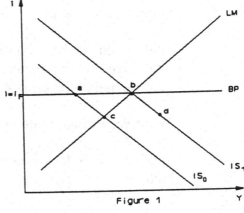

Figure 1

8. In the economy depicted in Figure 1, external balance is achieved at

a. points a or b.
b. only point b.
c. points b or c.
d. only point c.

9. In the economy depicted in Figure 1, internal and external balance is achieved at

a. points a or b.
b. points b or c.
c. only point b.
d. only point c.

10. The Mundell-Fleming model considers equilibrium in

a. an open economy with floating exchange rates and perfect capital mobility.
b. an open economy with floating exchange rates and sluggish capital flows.
c. an open economy with fixed exchange rates and perfect capital mobility.
d. a closed economy.

True or False?

T F 1. With fixed exchange rates, a country is unable to undertake independent monetary policy.

T F 2. The BP curve will be horizontal when all financial assets are perfect substitutes and capital is instantly mobile.

T F 3. Crowding out never occurs in the Mundell-Fleming model.

T F 4. With fixed exchange rates, expansionary monetary policy will be effectively neutralized when the central bank sells reserves for domestic currency in order to maintain the exchange rate.

T F 5. With fixed exchange rates, expansionary fiscal policy will increase output and income.

T F 6. With flexible exchange rates, expansionary monetary policy will increase output and income.

T F 7. Under a system of fixed exchange rates, expansionary fiscal policy will force the central bank to buy foreign exchange with domestic currency.

T F   8.   National income will fall if consumers decide to devote a larger fraction of their expenditures to imports.

Matching

For this exercise, use the IS-LM-BP analysis as illustrated in Figure 2 at the right. Each answer may be used more than once.

a.   the IS curve shifts to the right
b.   the IS curve shifts to the left
c.   the LM curve shifts to the right
d.   the LM curve shifts to the left
e.   the BP curve moves upward
f.   the BP curve moves downward
g.   there is no effect

Indicate the initial effect of each of the following policies.

____1. The government unexpectedly decreases the money supply.

____2. The domestic currency depreciates relative to its trading partners' currencies.

____3. Bad news: taxes go up.

____4. The government moves from a balanced domestic budget to a budget deficit.

____5. The currencies of the country's trading partners depreciates relative to the domestic currency.

____6. The central bank loosens its tight money policy.

____7. It's an election year and taxes are cut.

____8. Congress finally balances the budget after a decade of deficit spending.

____9. Governments coordinate policies: all exchange rates float, and taxes are cut simultaneously.

Answers

Chapter 1

Define and/or Explain

Gross National Product (GNP): The value of new goods and services produced by a country's nationals, regardless of where they are located.

Gross Domestic Product (GDP): The value of new goods and services produced within the boundaries of a country, no matter whether they are produced by foreign or domestic factors.

Exports: Goods sold by economic agents located in one country to economic agents located in another country.

Imports: Goods purchased by economic agents located in one country from economic agents located in another country.

Index of Openness: A measure of the importance of international trade to an economy or country, calculated as the ratio of exports to GNP or GDP.

Trade Deficit: A country has a trade deficit if its merchandise imports are greater than its merchandise exports.

Trade Surplus: A country has a trade surplus if its merchandise exports are greater than its merchandise imports.

Multiple Choice		True or False?	
1.	e	1.	F
2.	b	2.	F
3.	c	3.	F
4.	d	4.	F
5.	a	5.	T
6.	b	6.	T
7.	c	7.	F
8.	d	8.	F
9.	d	9.	T
10.	c	10.	F

Chapter 2

Define and/or Explain

positive analysis: Analysis that studies economic behavior without making recommendations about what is or ought to be.

normative analysis: Economic analysis that makes value judgements regarding what is or should be.

general equilibrium: Simultaneous equilibrium in all of the markets of an economy.

money illusion: A situation where people change spending habits when their incomes change, even when prices change by an equal (proportional) amount.

relative price: A ratio of two product prices.

nominal price: A price expressed in terms of money.

production possibility frontier: A diagram which shows the maximum amount of one type of good that can be produced in an economy, given the production of the other.

opportunity cost: The amount of production of one type of good which must be sacrificed in order to produce one more unit of the other.

indifference curve: A diagram which expresses the consumption preferences of an individual consumer.

community indifference curves: A diagram which expresses the preferences of all of the consumers of a country.

autarky: A situation where a country does not take part in international trade.

national supply: The amount of national output of a particular good at various relative prices for that good.

national demand: The amount of demand for a particular good at various relative prices.

Multiple Choice	**True or False?**	**Matching**
1. d	1. T	1. c
2. d	2. F	2. e
3. c	3. F	3. d
4. a	4. T	4. j
5. b	5. F	5. f
6. b	6. T	6. h
7. a	7. T	7. g
8. b	8. F	8. b
9. c	9. T	9. i
10. a	10. F	10. a
11. c		
12. c		
13. b		
14. d		
15. a		

Chapter 3

Define and/or Explain

Division of labor: the assignment of labor to specific tasks in the production process.

Mercantilism: a system of government policies and institutions aimed at increasing exports and decreasing imports.

Constant returns to scale: a technological relationship such that proportionate changes in inputs leads to a proportionate change in output.

Absolute advantage: the ability of a country to produce a good using fewer productive inputs than is possible anywhere else in the world.

Comparative advantage: A country has comparative advantage in a good if the product has a lower pre-trade price relative price ratio than is found elsewhere in the world.

Terms of trade: the relative price at which trade occurs between countries.

Consumption possibilities frontier: the various bundles of goods which a country can obtain by taking advantage of international trade.

Trade triangle: a geometric device which tells us the amounts a country is willing to trade at a particular world price.

Walras' Law: all markets will be in equilibrium if all but one already is.

Reciprocal demand: the process of international interaction of demand and supply necessary to produce an international price.

Importance of being unimportant: when small countries trade with big countries, the small are likely to enjoy most of the mutual gains from trade.

Over and under valued currencies: a currency is under (over) valued if the price of foreign money (the exchange rate) is too high (low) to permit balanced international trade.

Multiple Choice		**True or False?**		**Matching**	
1.	c	1.	T	1.	h
2.	d	2.	F	2.	c
3.	a	3.	F	3.	i
4.	d	4.	T	4.	d
5.	b	5.	T	5.	j
6.	a	6.	F	6.	a
7.	d	7.	T	7.	b
8.	c	8.	F	8.	g
9.	c	9.	T	9.	e
10.	a	10.	T	10.	f
11.	a				
12.	b				
13.	a				
14.	a				
15.	d				
16.	b				
17.	b				
18.	d				
19.	a				
20.	c				

Chapter 4

Define and/or Explain

factor endowments: The quantities of factors of production (e.g. labor and machines) possessed by a country.

labor (capital) intensive: A good is labor (capital) intensive relative to another good if its production requires more (less) labor per machine than the other good requires in its production.

labor (capital) abundant: A country is labor (capital abundant relative to another country if it has more (less) workers per machine than the other country.

incomplete specialization: A country is incompletely specialized in production if, after trade begins, it continues to produce some of the good it imports.

factor price equalization: Factor price equalization occurs if all individual factor prices (e.g. wages, rental payments) are identical when measured in the same currency.

Multiple Choice		True or False?		Matching	
1.	c	1.	F	1.	b
2.	b	2.	T	2.	c
3.	d	3.	T	3.	h
4.	d	4.	F	4.	f
5.	d	5.	F	5.	i
6.	b	6.	F	6.	a
7.	a	7.	F	7.	j
8.	d	8.	T	8.	e
9.	b	9.	T		
10.	c	10.	T		
11.	a				
12.	a				

Chapter 5

Define and/or Explain

input-output table: A table which details the sales of one industry to all other industries in an economy.

Leontief Paradox: The finding that US imports are produced using relatively capital intensive techniques.

product life cycle: The process by which a product is invented and then over time becomes more standardized as consumers and producers gain familiarity with its features.

intraindustry trade: The simultaneous import and export of similar types of products by a country.

increasing returns to scale: A technological situation where proportionate increases in the use of productive inputs leads to greater than proportionate increases in output.

Multiple Choice		True or False?	
1.	c	1.	F
2.	d	2.	F
3.	b	3.	T
4.	c	4.	F
5.	c	5.	T
6.	c	6.	F
7.	a	7.	T
8.	c	8.	T
9.	b	9.	F
10.	d	10.	F
11.	b		
12.	d		

Chapter 6

Define and/or Explain

commercial policy: Policies taken by a government to influence the quantity and composition of that country's international trade.

tariff: Tax imposed by a government either on exports or imports.

quota: A government mandated limitation on either the quantity or value of trade in a product.

subsidy: A government payment to industry based upon the amount it engages in international trade.

non-tariff barriers: A wide range of government policies other than tariffs designed to affect the volume or composition of international trade of that country.

static gains from trade: Increases in economic well-being, holding the resources and technology constant, that accrue to a country that engages in international trade.

dynamic gains from trade: Increases in economic well being that accrue to an economy because trade expands the resources of a country or induces increases in the productivity of existing resources.

political gains from trade: Increases in economic well-being that accrue to a country because expanded trade and economic interdependency may increase the likelihood of reduced international hostility.

ad valorem tariff: A tax equal to a given percentage of the selling price.

specific tariff: A tax equal to a fixed amount of money per unit sold.

compound tariff: A tax that has both a specific and an ad valorem component.

revenue effect: The amount of revenue accruing to the government from a tariff.protective effect: The amount that domestic producers are able to expand their output because the tariff is in place.

Most Favored Nation (MFN) status: A country confers MFN upon another country be agreeing not to charge tariffs on that country's goods that are any higher than those it imposes on the goods of any other country.

Generalized System of Preferences (GSP): A system where industrialized countries charge preferential (lower) tariff rates on goods from certain developing countries.

consumer surplus: The difference between the amount consumers are willing to pay to purchase a given quantity of goods and the amount they have to pay to purchase those goods.

producer surplus: The difference between the price paid in the market for a good and the minimum price required by an industry to produce and market that unit.

deadweight cost of the tariff: The value of wasted resources devoted to expanded domestic production and expenditures devoted to less desired substitutes brought about by a tariff.

optimal tariff: The size of the tariff that raises the tariff imposing country's welfare by the greatest amount relative to free trade welfare levels.

trade war: A general reduction in world trade brought about by increases in trade barriers throughout the world.

average tariff: A measure of the height of a country's tariff barriers.

effective rate of protection: The amount of protection provided to the domestic content of a product by the tariff structure of a country.

tariff escalation: Tariff rates that rise with stages of processing. (Sometimes called cascading tariffs.)

Multiple Choice		**True or False?**	
1.	a	1.	T
2.	a	2.	F
3.	c	3.	F
4.	a	4.	F
5.	d	5.	T
6.	c	6.	F
7.	c	7.	F
8.	b	8.	T
9.	a	9.	F
10.	c	10.	F
11.	a		
12.	d		
13.	d		
14.	b		
15.	a		
1.	c		
17.	a		
18.	d*		
19.	b		
20.	c		
21.	d		
22.	d		
23.	c		

*note: $(i+j)-(i+j+k+m+n)+(m)= -\$(k+n)$. \$r is a loss in efficient production that affects world welfare.

Chapter 7

Define and/or Explain

quota: Government imposed limitation on the volume or value of international trade.

embargo: A complete ban on trade in a product or products.

quota rents: Profits that come about because a quota has artificially raised the price of imported products.

voluntary export restraint: An agreement reached between importing and exporting countries whereby the exporters agree to limit the amount they export.

export subsidy: A payment by a government to an industry that leads to an expansion of exports by that country.

countervailing duty: A tax imposed by an importing country designed to offset artificially low prices charged by exporters.

Buy American Acts: Laws that direct purchasing agents of U.S. federal, state, and local governments to purchase American made products unless comparable foreign goods are substantially cheaper.

infant industry argument: Argument that says that new industries may need temporary protection until they have mastered the production and marketing techniques necessary to be competitive in the world market.

Multiple Choice		**True or False?**	
1.	b	1.	F
2.	d	2.	T
3.	c	3.	F
4.	b	4.	T
5.	a	5.	T
6.	d	6.	F
7.	c	7.	F
8.	d	8.	F
9.	b	9.	T
10.	a	10.	F
11.	d		
12.	a		
13.	c		
14.	d		
15.	b		

Chapter 8

Define and/or Explain

logrolling: The trading of votes by legislators in order to secure approval on issues of interest (such as tariffs) to each one.

unconditional most favored nation status: The principle of nondiscrimination in international trade.

dumping: Selling a product in a foreign market at a price that is below fair market value.

predatory dumping: Dumping in order to drive foreign competitors out of their market so that the market can then be monopolized.

international price discrimination: Selling a product in two different countries at two different prices.

dumping margin: The difference between the market price of a product and its fair market value.

injury test: An investigation to determine whether an unfair foreign trade practice has caused or threatens to cause harm to a domestic industry.

countervailing duty: A tariff designed to raise the price of an imported product to its fair market value.

upstream subsidies: A subsidy that lowers the cost of an input for a manufacturer.

Section 301: A provision in US trade law that requires the US government to negotiate the elimination of foreign unfair trade practices and to retaliate against these countries if negotiations fail.

escape clause: A measure in US trade law that allows for temporary protection against fairly traded foreign imports.

trade adjustment assistance: Payments made by the government to help factors retrain or retool after they have been displaced by foreign competition.

safeguards protection: General name for measures such as the escape clause that provide protection to local firms from fairly traded foreign goods.

Multiple Choice		**True or False?**		**Matching**	
1	a	1.	F	1.	e
2.	b	2.	F	2.	a
3.	b	3.	T	3.	d
4.	a	4.	F	4.	f
5.	d	5.	F	5.	b
6.	a	6.	F	6.	c
7.	c	7.	F		
8.	a	8.	T		
9.	d	9.	F		
10.	b	10.	T		
11.	c				
12.	b				
13.	d				

Chapter 9

Define and/or Explain

free trade area: An agreement between countries to eliminate internal trade barriers but to give each member the right to decide its own trade policy against nonmember countries.

customs union: An agreement between countries to eliminate internal trade barriers and to adopt a common external trade policy.

trade diversion: A shift in the pattern of trade from a low cost world producer to a higher cost producer within the preferential trading area.

trade creation: An expansion in world trade resulting from the formation of a preferential trading agreement.

North American Free Trade Agreement: An agreement to establish a free trade area between Canada, the United States and Mexico.

rules of origin: Rules regarding the national identity of products necessary in discriminatory trade agreements.

Single European Act: Directed EU members to establish common technical standards and to eliminate regulatory barriers to internal trade.

Maastricht Agreement: Laid out specific steps for EU countries to form a monetary union with a single currency.

Multiple Choice		True or False?	
1.	b	1.	T
2.	c	2.	T
3.	b	3.	F
4.	b	4.	T
5.	b	5.	T
6.	c	6.	F
7.	d	7.	T
8.	d	8.	T
9.	a		
10.	d		

Chapter 10

Define and/or Explain

economic development: The process of achieving a high quality of life for the average citizen. This would include adequate housing and health care, as well as broad educational attainment.

primary export-led growth: Economic growth driven by production and export of natural resources and land intensive products.

import substitution policies: Policies such as tariffs and quotas that encourage domestic production as a replacement for imports.

outward looking development strategy: A growth plan emphasizing open markets, decontrol of wages and prices, and the development of industries in the which the country has a potential comparative advantage.

neutral growth: Proportionate increase in all factors and consumption so that trade expands proportionately to the growth of the economy.

pro-trade biased growth: Growth that results in an expansion of trade that exceeds the rate of growth of GNP.

anti-trade biased growth: Growth that results in a reduction of trade relative to the size of the economy.

neutral technological change: An innovation that results in an equi-proportionate use of all factors in the production of one unit of output.

labor saving technical change: An innovation that results in a more than proportionate reduction in the use of labor relative to other factors in the production of one unit of output.

immizerizing growth: Economic growth that results in a reduction in national economic welfare.

guest workers: Foreign workers who are invited to temporarily relocate in a country in order to work in a certain sector of an economy.

brain drain: The permanent relocation of skilled workers from one country to another.

multinational corporation: A corporation that operates production or marketing facilities in more than one country.

marginal product of labor: The additional amount of output (in physical terms) that is produced because one more worker is added to the production process.

diminishing returns to labor: The phenomenon that as workers are added to the production process, holding all other factors fixed, the marginal product of labor declines.

value marginal product of labor: The monetary value of the marginal product of labor.

Multiple Choice		**True or False?**	
1.	d	1.	F
2.	d	2.	T
3.	a	3.	T
4.	d	4.	T
5.	e	5.	T
6.	a	6.	F
7.	d	7.	F
8.	c	8.	F
9.	c	9.	T
10	c	10.	T
11.	d		
12.	b		
13.	a		
14.	b		
15.	d		
16.	b		
17.	a		

Chapter 11

Define and/or Explain

balance of payments: The record of a country's international transactions with the rest of the world.
trade deficit: Merchandise imports exceed exports.
trade surplus: Merchandise exports exceed imports.
exchange rate: The price of one money in terms of another
foreign exchange market: The global market where currencies are traded.
purchasing power parity: Similar goods sell for the same price in two different countries, when price is measured in a common currency.

Multiple Choice		**True or False?**	
1.	d	1.	F
2.	a	2.	F
3.	c	3.	F
4.	c	4.	T
5.	d	5.	F
6.	d	6.	T
7.	b	7.	T
8.	c	8.	F

Chapter 12

Define and/or Explain

deficit (surplus): Balance of payments debit items exceed (are less than) the credit items in value.

balance of trade: The value of merchandise exports minus imports.

basic balance: The current account plus long-term capital.

liquidity balance: The basic balance plus short-term capital and errors and omissions.

official settlements balance: The value of the change in short-term capital held by foreign monetary agencies and official reserve asset transactions.

balance of payments equilibrium: Credits equal debits for a particular account.

flexible exchange rates: Free market supply and demand determines the value of currencies.

fixed exchange rates: Central banks peg exchange rates at desired levels.

Multiple Choice		**True or False?**	
1.	e	1.	T
2.	b	2.	F
3	c	3.	F
4.	a	4.	F
5.	d	5.	F
6.	a	6.	T
7.	b	7.	T
8.	c	8.	T
9.	c	9.	T
10.	c	10.	F
11.	a		
12.	c		
13.	a		

Matching

1. c j The interest is recorded in investment income (credit) while the matching entry is (debit) in short-term capital.

2. i l The new plant is long-term direct foreign investment, so long-term capital is debited and the matching entry is a credit to short-term capital due to a decrease in US-owned bank deposits abroad.

3. i h The bank account is an increase in foreign-owned bank deposits in the United States so credit short-term capital. The balancing entry is a debit to unilateral transfers since the money was foreign aid.

4. a j The tractors are US exports, and so a merchandise credit. The decrease in foreign-owned US bank deposits represents a debit to short-term capital.

5. i j The bond purchase is a short-term (less than a year) capital inflow (credit) balanced by a decrease of foreign-owned deposits in US banks, a short-term capital debit.

Chapter 13

Define and/or Explain

exchange rate: The price of one money in terms of another.

spread: The difference between the buying and selling price of a currency.

spot market: Where currencies are traded for current delivery.

cross rate: The third exchange rate implied by any two exchange rates involving three currencies.

depreciate: The value of one currency falls relative to another.

appreciate: The value of one currency rises relative to another.

forward exchange market: Where currencies may be bought and sold for delivery in a future period.

forward premium: Forward exchange rate exceeds the spot rate.

forward discount: Forward exchange rate is less than the spot rate.

currency swap: An agreement to trade currencies at one date and reverse the trade at a later date.

hedging: An activity to offset risk.

margin: A deposit with a broker required for trading in the futures market.

call: An option to buy currency.

put: An option to sell currency.

striking price: The price of currency stated in an option contract.

black market: An illegal market in foreign exchange.

parallel market: A free market allowed to coexist with the official market.

Multiple Choice		True or False?	
1.	b	1.	T
2.	c	2.	T
3.	d	3.	F
4.	a	4.	T
5.	a	5.	F
6.	c	6.	T
7.	b	7.	T
8.	c	8.	F
9.	a	9.	T
10.	a+b+c+d	10.	F

Chapter 14

Define and/or Explain

nominal: A value dependent on current price levels.

law of one price: Similar goods sell for the same price worldwide.

relative price change: The price of one good relative to another good changes.

random: Moving in an unpredictable manner.

endogenous: A variable whose value is determined by some given factors.

exogenous: A variable whose value is given to the economic system by an outside force like government or nature.

shock: An unexpected change.

news: Unexpected information.

spurious: Not a true relationship.

Multiple Choice		True or False?		Matching	
1.	c	1.	F	1., 2.	c and e
2.	b	2.	T	3., 4.	b and d
3.	c	3.	F	5., 6.	a and f
4.	d	4.	F		
5.	a	5.	T		
6.	e	6.	F		
7.	a	7.	T		
8.	b	8.	F		
9.	a	9.	F		
10.	d	10.	T		
11.	c				

Chapter 15

Define and/or Explain

covered return: Domestic currency value of a foreign investment when the foreign currency proceeds are sold in the forward market.

interest rate parity (covered): The forward premium or discount is equal to the interest differential.

effective return: The foreign interest rate plus the forward premium or discount.

interest rate parity (uncovered): The expected change in the exchange rate is equal to the interest differential.

nominal interest rate: The rate actually observed in the market.

real interest rate: Nominal interest rate minus inflation.

Fisher equation: The nominal interest rate is equal to the real interest rate plus expected inflation.

term structure of interest rates: The pattern of interest rates over different terms to maturity.

Multiple Choice		True or False?	
1.	b	1.	F
2.	a	2.	T
3.	b	3.	T
4.	b	4.	T
5.	d	5.	F
6.	c	6.	F
7.	c	7.	T
8.	a	8.	F
9.	d	9.	F
10.	b	10.	T
11.	a	11.	T
12.	b	12.	F
13.	c		
14.	d		
15.	b		

Chapter 16

Define and/or Explain

exchange risk exposure: Translation, transactions, and economic exposure are three concepts of exposure to foreign exchange risk.

risk premium: Difference between the forward rate and the expected future spot rate.

risk aversion: The tendency of investors to prefer less risk.

efficient market: Prices reflect all available information.

short position: Selling currency for future delivery.

long position: Buying currency for future delivery.

diversified portfolios: Holding a mix of assets denominated in several currencies.

variance: Measures the dispersion of a variable about its mean value.

covariance: Measures how two variables fluctuate about their means together.

systematic risk: Risk common to all investments.

nonsystematic risk: Risk that can be eliminated with diversification.

capital flight: Large capital outflows resulting from unfavorable investment conditions in a country.

Multiple Choice		True or False?	
1.	a	1.	T
2.	c	2.	T
3.	d	3.	F
4.	e	4.	F
5.	c	5.	F
6.	b	6.	T
7.	a	7.	F
8.	c	8.	F
9.	b	9.	T
10.	b	10.	F
11.	c		
12.	a		
13.	b		
14.	d		
15.	d		
16.	c		
17.	a		
18.	b		

Chapter 17

Define and/or Explain

relative price: The price of one good relative to the price of another good.

elasticity: The responsiveness of quantity to changes in price.

J-curve effect: Following a devaluation, the balance of trade falls for a while before increasing.

currency contract period: Period immediately following a devaluation when contracts signed prior to the devaluation are settled.

pass-through: The adjustment of domestic and foreign prices to devaluation.

pricing to market: Lowering the domestic currency price of exports in response to a currency appreciation to keep exported goods competitively priced in foreign markets.

absorption: Total domestic spending.

adjustment mechanism: The process by which international disequilibria are eliminated.

base money: Equals international reserves plus domestic credit.

domestic credit: Domestic component of base money.

international reserves: Portion of base money used to settle international debts.

small open economy: Cannot affect the international price of goods or the foreign interest rate.

Multiple Choice		True or False?	
1.	a	1.	F
2.	c	2.	T
3.	b	3.	T
4.	a	4.	T
5.	b	5.	F
6.	c	6.	F
7.	d	7.	T
8.	b	8.	F
9.	c	9.	F
10.	c	10.	T
11.	a	11.	T
		12.	F
		13.	F

Chapter 18

Define and/or Explain

perfect capital mobility: No barriers to international capital flows.
portfolio balance approach: A theory of exchange rate determination that argues that the exchange rate is a function of relative supplies of domestic and foreign bonds.
sterilized intervention: A foreign exchange market intervention combined with a domestic open market operation that leaves the domestic money supply unchanged.
currency union: An agreement between countries to fix exchange rates and coordinate monetary policies.

Multiple Choice		**True or False?**	
1.	b	1.	F
2.	a+d	2.	F
3.	a	3.	T
4.	c	4.	T
5.	b	5.	T
6.	d	6.	F
7.	a	7.	F
8.	b	8.	T
9.	d	9.	T
10.	c	10.	T
11.	a		
12.	b		
13.	d		

Chapter 19

Define and/or Explain

gold standard: Currencies have fixed values in terms of gold.
commodity money standard: The value of money is fixed relative to a commodity.
SDR: An international reserve asset created by the IMF.
EMS: A monetary union of European countries.
ERM: Requires EU countries to keep their exchange rates within narrow bands.
Maastricht Treaty: Agreement for Europe to have a single currency by the end of the century.
crawling peg: Exchange rate is fixed for a time and then adjusted at regular intervals.
destabilizing speculation: Speculators increase the variability of exchange rates.
seigniorage: The difference between the exchange value of a money and its cost of production.
ECU: A composite currency unit created by the EMS.

Multiple Choice		True or False?	
1.	b	1.	T
2.	a	2.	T
3.	d	3.	F
4.	c	4.	F
5.	d	5.	F
6.	a	6.	T
7.	a	7.	F
8.	c	8.	F
9.	b	9.	T
10.	d	10.	F
11.	a	11.	T
12.	e	12.	F
13.	f	13.	F
14.	a		
15.	b		
16.	b		
17.	c		
18.	c		
19.	c		
20.	b		
21.	d		
22.	c		
23.	c		
24.	b		

Chapter 20

Define and/or Explain

Eurocurrency market: The deposit and loan of currencies outside of their domestic banking regulations.

LIBOR: London Interbank Offer Rate--the key interest rate in the Eurocurrency market.

IBFs: International Banking Facilities--international banking divisions of onshore US banks.

petrodollars: Eurodollar deposits arising from OPEC trade surpluses.

Paris Club: A gathering of creditor country governments to arrange debt rescheduling.

debt-equity swap: An exchange of developing country debt for an ownership position in a developing country business.

Multiple Choice		True or False?		Matching	
1.	a	1.	F	1.	f
2.	f	2.	F	2.	g
3.	c	3.	T	3.	c
4.	c	4.	F	4.	d
5.	b	5.	F	5.	e
6.	d	6.	T	6.	a
7.	b	7.	F	7.	j
8.	a	8.	F	8.	i
9.	b	9.	T	9.	h
10.	d	10.	T	10.	b

Chapter 21

Define and/or Explain

internal balance: Achieving economic growth consistent with a low unemployment rate.
external balance: Achieving a desired trade or capital account balance.
IS curve: Combinations of i and Y that provide equilibrium in the goods market.
LM curve: Combinations of i and Y that provide equilibrium in the money market.
BP curve: Combinations of i and Y that provide equilibrium in the balance of payments.
Mundell-Fleming model: The IS-LM-BP model with flexible exchange rates and perfect capital mobility.
crowding out: An increase in government speding is offset by a reduction in private spending such as net exports.
open economy multiplier: Equals the reciprocal of the marginal propensity to save plus the marginal propensity to import.

Multiple Choice		**True or False?**		**Matching**	
1.	d	1.	T	1.	d
2.	b	2.	T	2.	a
3.	c	3.	F	3.	b
4.	a	4.	T	4.	a
5.	f	5.	T	5.	b
6.	d	6.	T	6.	c
7.	c	7.	T	7.	a
8.	a	8.	T	8.	b
9.	c			9.	a+e
10.	a